Ron Paul is Right:
Rick Perry is
No Conservative

Ron Paul is Right: Rick Perry is No Conservative

Why the U.S. Political System is Failing and the New Fight for the American Dream

June Melton, III
An Opinion Piece

Martin & Byrd Books, LLC • Lakeway
2011

Published in the United States by
Martin & Byrd Books, LLC
P.O. Box 342253
Lakeway, TX 78734

ISBN 978-0-9826519-2-6

Library of Congress Control Number: 2011944473

Printed in the United States of America

Second Edition

Cover Photo: "Rick Perry" © 2011 Gage Skidmore. Used by permission.

To America's Youth
Who will not have the opportunities that my generation had
unless they vote wisely.

CONTENTS

Introduction   ix
1   Imagine   1
2   The Conservative Candidate   8
3   The Perry "Enemies List" and the Patriot Act   17
4   Education, Jobs, and a Kickback to the Wealthy   29
5   Weird Wizards and Talk of Treason   37
6   The National Economy and the Fed's Insider   45
    Trading Apparatus
7   Paul Volcker, The George Bushes, and the   55
    Mexican Mafia
8   Fear and Loathing in the Media   65
9   Cash, Corruption, and Corporatism   73
10 Does Your NAFTA Doctor Speak English?   82
11 Buildings and Bridges Don't Simply Fall Down   94
12 Governor Rick Perry's "Trans-Texas Corridor"   113
    and the North American Union
13 Impeachable Moments – Three Days in March   127
14 Convention Notes   134
15 An American Spring   144
    Appendix   151
    End Notes/Bibliographical References   155

❧ INTRODUCTION ☙

I am a member of the "older generation." I wrote this book to help others of my generation understand why they should embrace the "Ron Paul movement."

From the 1970s into the early 1980s I owned a medium-sized design/engineering/construction firm in Midland, Texas. At its peak, I employed 15 people full time and a very large number of young people part time. I was able to mentor young architects and engineers, which I enjoyed doing very much. Now I employ only a few people I deeply trust, choosing to subcontract to other small firms many of the necessary skills needed for me to run an engineering firm.

What changed for me? I happened to be a witness to fraud and insider dealing among some of the Forbes richest Americans—directors of the First National Bank of Midland. I was also a witness to how the Federal Reserve deliberately manipulated that bank into failure, with the directors getting away with their fortunes by cutting secret deals with government officials; while thousands of stockholders lost their retirement incomes as FDIC "storm troopers" took over the bank. One federal judge termed the government's actions: "Star Chamber Hitlerian tactics." It was the beginning of "too big to fail" and loss of individual liberties and contract rights to a statist system that plague the nation today.

I saw the Federal Reserve continuing its unconstitutional attack on the nation, destroying banks and seizing assets throughout Texas, Oklahoma, and the nation's heartland—from coast to coast. Millions suffered during the 1980s; untold numbers of Americans died; but the media published the opposite effect in order to protect the Federal

Reserve. Those who made money were able to take advantage of the 1980 Monetary Control Act signed into law by President Carter that abolished states-rights in banking and imposed usury on the nation. That is how the financial elite grew in power at the expense of the other 99 percent, and why credit card interest rates still exceed 10 percent in spite of today's bad economy.

I grew up in Midland and, during the 1950s, lived in the same neighborhood as the George H.W. Bush family. I knew George W. well and would invite him to play baseball; but for almost 60 years I have also witnessed that family's increasingly worrisome lust for power and money. I even naively worked on their campaigns to higher office. In this book I mention their involvement in dishonest banking practices and the impact on President Ronald Reagan in dealing with then-Federal Reserve Chairman Paul Volcker. I also discuss a January, 2008 alliance between Volcker and then-candidate Barack Obama—an alliance that meant that the Federal Reserve was "sending a message" for Wall Street to support Obama for the presidency, ultimately enabling AIG executives to get their bonuses.

Now the nation is witnessing another presidential campaign. In January 2012, with the "no-to-Mitt Romney" voters consistently in the majority, and Florida polls showing Romney having less than 50% support, former President George H. W. Bush and Midland-born son Jeb Bush headed to Washington, D.C. for the purpose, I suspect, of trying to achieve an alliance with President Obama. Such an alliance could "send a message" to Wall Street—the same tactic used by the Federal Reserve in January 2008—and Obama would serve out a second term in 2012, with Jeb Bush then "anointed" president in 2016. Two days after that meeting, it was learned that Wall Street executives were abandoning Romney and will be quietly donating one billion dollars to the Obama campaign. After all, Wall Street executives have greatly profited during the current recession (even more than they had profited under the previous Bush administration) because the Obama Justice Department has driven the number of financial-fraud investigations down to a 20-year low.

In the early 1990s, evidently as a result of the Federal Reserve's attack on the Texas banking system, Congressman Henry B. González

(D-TX), who chaired the House Banking Committee, ordered an investigation of the Federal Reserve. The Fed fiercely resisted; however, the Committee was able to determine that the Federal Reserve is perhaps the largest insider trading operation in the world, which I discuss in this book. Congressman Ron Paul was not in Congress at that particular point in time, but when Paul ran again for Congress in 1995, then-House Speaker Newt Gingrich and then-Governor George W. Bush did everything possible to try to prevent Paul's election, evidently to protect the Federal Reserve from being audited and try to prevent Ron Paul from being heard from the floor of the House.

I became an elected Texas GOP precinct delegate in 2008, and I personally witnessed the GOP establishment committing fraud against delegates who supported the message of Congressman Ron Paul. I write about that experience in one of the chapters in this book. Now in 2012, allegations of fraud committed by the GOP hierarchy against Ron Paul voters have again surfaced, with ballot boxes missing in early primary states, forcing the resignation of GOP chairs in two states. In Iowa, influential members of the Republican establishment stand accused of offering sweetheart deals to leaders in key swing districts, to "sway" the results so that Ron Paul would not win, thereby depriving Iowa voters of their sacred right to vote and be represented by a particular candidate.

I write about my personal experience in trying to run my small engineering business in the age of government spying through the banking system; and how, using the Patriot Act the government secretly breaks into business facilities without a search warrant, to copy or steal business records.

Ron Paul speaks of the dangers of "corporatism" and the importance of fair trade. I write about the destructive nature of both corporatism and NAFTA. No US president has had to go to Congress to declare war since World War II and no bankrupt nation is able to maintain a national defense. The experience of the Soviet Union should serve as a reminder to members of my generation. Ten years of war have cost this nation over $3.7 trillion, with over 6000 US soldiers killed and 550,000 VA disability claims filed, which might explain why individual members of the military contribute more money to the Ron Paul campaign than to all the other candidates combined.

The older generation fears for the future of its children and grandchildren and knows what this nation has lost during our lifetimes. There are solutions to many of the problems that plague this nation, several of which I offer in this book; however, it takes education, especially the education of many of the nation's elderly who vote mainly based on what they hear from politically-biased TV. But the elderly also do not appreciate being lied to, and are sick and tired of the nation being held in such contempt by other nations in the world. They could switch their allegiances to Ron Paul if given good enough reasons for doing so; but they need to learn and vote during the primaries in order to have any meaningful effect. Ron Paul says: "we need to change hearts and minds." Ron Paul is Right. From this member of the older generation, that is the purpose of this book.

— June Melton

1

⧼ IMAGINE ⧽

Imagine there's no countries, it isn't hard to do.
~ "Imagine" by John Lennon 1940-1980

Americans need to learn everything they can, very soon, about Republican Congressman Ron Paul. Paul is running for the presidency of the United States in 2012 to save the Republic and the nation's Constitution. Unlike most of the others running, Ron Paul is not in politics to increase his personal wealth and power. Since Congressman Paul is actually the only "non-establishment, non-status quo" candidate in the race, he is actually the only true "conservative."

Americans already know as much as they care to know about current President Barack Obama. America is in a serious financial crisis. When it comes to summing up the financial condition of the United States, Jeffrey T. Kuhner said it best in the August 11, 2011 edition of *The Washington Times*:

> "America's economy is in free-fall. Growth is anemic. The stock market is collapsing. Real unemployment—combining the high jobless rate with rampant underemployment—is higher than 16 percent. Manufacturing is dead. Deficits, debt and government spending are at record levels. Our credit rating has been downgraded for the first time in history. The trade deficit has exploded to the highest in years. A possible Great Depression haunts the land. Primarily one man is to blame: President Obama.

"Mr. Obama has racked up more than $4 trillion in debt. His massive spending stimulus has failed and made the jobless situation worse. Before his stimulus package was passed in February 2009, the unemployment rate stood at 7.8 percent. Today it is at 9.1 percent—and rising. Mr. Obama promised that his Keynesian borrow-and-spend policies would kick-start the economy. He has run up three consecutive trillion-dollar-plus budget deficits, an orgy of spending unrivaled in our history. The result: Nearly 2 million private-sector jobs have been wiped out, the U.S. dollar has eroded, investor and business confidence has been shattered, and America is no longer the world's economic superpower. Washington has become a financial colony of China.

"Under Mr. Obama, America's decline has been swift, sudden and stunning—almost bewildering. Even many liberals are beginning to turn on him. The New York Times and liberal columnists such as Maureen Dowd and Eleanor Clift are attacking him relentlessly. The media establishment is in panic. The mainstream press portrayed him in 2008 as a world historical figure who combined Abraham Lincoln, John F. Kennedy, Martin Luther King Jr. and Mahatma Gandhi—a progressive messiah who would heal racial wounds at home and restore peace abroad. Some even compared him to God. Now many of these same journalists have come to a shocking conclusion: Mr. Obama is morphing into Jimmy Carter. They are staring at another failed liberal presidency. Yet the damage is much worse than what happened under the Carter administration."

On June 15, 2011, to keep the government from going further into debt, prevent the bankruptcy of Medicare, and protect America's seniors, U.S. Sen. John Cornyn, (R-TX), a member of the Senate Finance Committee, led the Senate Republican Conference in a letter to President Obama, stating that the Administration stands in violation of federal law, section 802 of P.L. 108-173, the Medicare Prescription Drug, Improvement and Modernization Act of 2003.

The letter asked the President to comply with federal law, by immediately submitting to Congress the Administration's legislative proposal for addressing the Medicare funding warning issued in the 2010 Medicare Trustees' Report. The letter stated in part, "The Medicare Trustees have complied with federal law and have issued funding warnings every year since 2007. In 2008, the Bush Administration, in compliance with Section 802 of the MMA, submitted a legislative proposal to Congress, which was never acted upon. Your Administration, however, has failed to submit such a proposal for the last three years."

No proposal came from the Obama Administration. When Obama warned that the debt ceiling must be raised by August 2, 2011 or the nation's Social Security retirees, military retirees, Social Security disability and federal retires would not get their checks, and the nation's credit rating would be lowered, a cowed-Congress raised the debt ceiling and then shirked its responsibilities further by establishing a committee to study the matter.

President Obama did not volunteer to stop payments to illegal aliens; eliminate frivolous benefits such as Internet access for violent inmates; fire some of the thousands of unnecessary highest paid federal employees that he had hired; volunteer to cut down on his or his wife's gallivanting around; stop payments to the senators and representatives or any of their staff; lower benefits to welfare recipients; restructure food stamp programs or stop foreign aid.

Credit rating agency Standard and Poor's then downgraded the nation's credit rating. Democrats were livid at the credit downgrade and blamed the "Tea Party" movement, while Hollywood celebrity and other entitled swells partied heartily at the White House during Obama's 50th birthday. With the economy collapsing, financial markets falling, and millions of Americans jobless, hurting, hungry and angry, the president danced barefooted as he gorged himself on barbecued ribs and sipped champagne.

Millions of Americans now recognize Mr. Obama as an establishment politician lacking the character, intelligence, experience, skills and basic competence to be the leader of the free world. However, with Obama's approval ratings among African-Americans and the hard core left-wing portion of the Democratic party still high, there has been no inclination on the part of Democrats to replace him with a more qualified candidate. Mr. Obama's reelection depends entirely on whom his republican opponent will be in the 2012 presidential elections, and now might be the time for unhappy democrats and independents to look at alternatives who are campaigning within the Republican Party -- mainly Ron Paul.

On August 13, 2011, another "non-conservative" -- Texas Governor Rick Perry -- after playing "will-he-won't-he run" and teasing the news media for months, glibly announced his presidential ambitions in South Carolina. Perry's race was now underway for the Republican presidential nomination against several other GOP hopefuls who were participating in the Iowa Straw Poll the same day. U.S. Rep. Michele Bachmann and U.S. Rep. Ron Paul eventually topped the others in Iowa. Perry came in close to last after conducting an expensive write-in campaign.

Soon after entering the race, Perry fell under attack from the left for his comments about Social Security and from the right for his immigration policies. Perry's seemingly incoherent comments in the early GOP debates gave time for former Federal Reserve official Herman Cain and former Massachusetts governor Mitt Romney to gain an upper hand with Republicans; but not necessarily gain the upper hand with conservative Republicans and other groups including "Occupy Wall Street" protestors and the "Tea-Party" groups. Soon Cain and Bachmann dropped out of the running -- then Perry dropped out as well. But one thing the Perry campaign revealed to the nation (and that was concealed by the mainstream media) was the fact that money from the Bilderberg Group had been funneled through Rick Perry to the Republican Party.

Now imagine fast forwarding to a day in October, 2012 three weeks before the elections.

The GOP had spoken and had selected its nominee at the Republican convention in Tampa Bay, Florida in August. Millions of Obama-weary American citizens have already been bombarded by telemarketing operations and with direct mail solicitations, and have responded with whatever money they could contribute to the campaign. As election-day approaches, much of this money has already been used to pay to the fundraisers and corporate media for advertisements.

Mr. Obama's reelection campaign organization has responded in kind. Democratic Super PACs have raised unlimited contributions from unions, billionaire individuals, environmentalists, Hollywood and sports celebrities, and large national and international corporations, to fill Mr. Obama's campaign coffers.

Imagine that, on this day in October, 2012, Hollywood has now just released a widely advertised and wildly acclaimed movie depicting Mr. Obama as a leader and decider in the U.S. military's elimination of terrorist Osama bin Laden. Hollywood critics, celebrities and media sources are raving about how the movie should receive an Academy Award. The recently reborn Acorn vote-fraud industry is accelerating its activities in the "battleground states" under another name. Foreign governments are funneling millions of dollars into various campaigns through straw-men American lawyers giving money to Super PACs. The airwaves are filled with demands that government and the rich create jobs; that the Republicans refuse to raise taxes on the rich; that corporations (including small businesses just barely getting by) must pay more; and that seniors will suffer greatly when Medicare and Social Security payments are cut by the Republicans. As a warning for seniors to vote for Democrats, the Social Security Administration has already scared seniors by delaying social security payments to the most desperate seniors for a few weeks—a violation of the Hatch Act—but the agency will claim later that the checks were lost in the mail.

In spite of economic reality, the steady drumbeat of anti-American, mainstream-news media redistributionist rhetoric finally begins to mute the fact that it is not the private sector, but instead it is the government that comprises the "greedy" with its insatiable appetite for government programs and higher taxes. With the November, 2012 elections now only three weeks away, Mr. Obama's job approval ratings are finally starting to rise in the polls. Over loud objections from Republicans and Democrats alike, Diebold voting machines in

Nevada, New Hampshire and other states are being fraudulently preprogrammed to skew voting results and assure that certain public officials will remain in power no matter how anyone votes.[1]

Suddenly, a quiet voice of reason arises out of the chaos. The voice is coming across the Atlantic from Israel. It's a voice that is saying: "Vote Ron Paul and let my people go once again! Stop meddling here and stop trying to buy influence by giving me money. Stop trying to be the all powerful Peace Maker and let us work out the problems here on our own! If we think Iran is a threat, we can handle it and we'll take the consequences. It's not America's problem and you can't afford another war." These are the words of Mr. Rafi Farber, a US citizen living in Karnei Shomron, Israel.

Farber continues: "Jews always feel a deep existential isolation and loneliness. 'As I see them from the mountain tops, gaze on them from the heights, this is a people that dwells alone, not counted among the Nations,' says Balaam of the People of Israel in Numbers 23:9. We still feel that loneliness. So we take the money. It's shameful, it's theft, it's destructive, it's morally wrong, and it makes people hate us for tying them into a conflict they have no business trying to solve. I wanted it to end and didn't trust any Israeli leader to give it up on his own, so I looked up more about Ron Paul."

"Ron Paul doesn't want to be President to 'give' me freedom. He doesn't own my freedom and he didn't give it to me. The only reason Ron Paul wants to be President is to stop punishing people for using their freedom that is rightfully theirs. He wants no power. This is clear to anyone who listens to him speak," Farber says.

"There are two kinds of human beings. Those who want power, and those who want freedom," Farber continues. "If you're a man who seeks freedom and you come into contact with a real human soul, you become instantly addicted. Once you get hooked on Ron Paul, you can no longer bear to listen to a man who wants power and you become instantly disgusted when he starts saying words. Before, they were just boring. Now they're revolting. Listening to Romney or Gingrich or Bush or Obama makes you sick... It's like a ghost flapping its ethereal tongue at you. You can't bear it...there's no soul in it. These are not free men. These are power men who try and attain power, to control others with spin and talking points and contradictory statements like 'I want to cut the budget and expand the military!' Slaves follow these one-liners like mobs, and follow each other from candidate to candidate. Slowly but surely, Ron Paul activates a few of the individual souls in the mob as they bob from snappy comeback to snappy comeback and he goes up in the polls."

But then Farber says: "Yet, we cannot expect every man woman and child to understand or get excited about the message of liberty. In fact, most just can't handle it. Being truly free is as terrifying as it is electrifying. The Bible tells us this very clearly in the story of the Exodus from Egypt.

"When Moses finally accepted the role of deliverer from God, he was assigned to say the following to my great-grandparents the Israelites:

'Therefore say to the Israelites: I am God. I will free you from the labors of the Egyptians and deliver you from their bondage. I will redeem you with an outstretched arm and with amazing signs. And I will take you to be My people and I will be your God, and you will know that I am the Lord who freed you from the labors of the Egyptians.' (Ex. 6:6-7)

"And what was my grandparents' response?

'And Moses told this to the people, but they didn't listen due to lack of spirit and cruel bondage.' (6:9)

"Not everyone can handle the message of freedom. It's too frightening for some people, and some are just too enslaved. Those are the people that despise Ron Paul, the same types who rebelled against Moses in the desert and attempted to go back to Egypt. Freedom is too much for them and they can't handle the Divine gift. They want and need someone to control them. Their souls have been too battered by slavery, taxation, and wars."

Is it too late? Will Americans listen to Moses' words in 2012 ? Will Americans listen to Ron Paul?

2

౭ THE CONSERVATIVE CANDIDATE ౷

A liberal is someone who feels a great debt to his fellow man, which debt he proposes to pay off with your money.
~ G. Gordon Liddy

Most of the people who vote in the United States, categorize themselves as being "conservative" which is why many candidates to higher office often try to "out-conservative" their opponents. The problem is that most people seemingly don't know what a conservative really is, and therefore are unable to accurately spot one in a crowd of politicians, all of whom claim to be conservative.

In August 2011, after Congressman Ron Paul had learned that Governor Perry had entered the race, Paul said: "I'm very pleased that he's coming in because he represents the status quo. And I feel like I'm sort of separated from the other candidates with my strong belief in liberty, limited government and a different foreign policy and wanting to deal with the Fed. So he'll just cut into all their votes."

What Dr. Paul seemed to be saying with his simple "one or two liner" comment was that the "status quo" today is a failed economic system based on a fiat currency, with inflation created by the Federal Reserve printing too much money, and that he knows his opponents will say one thing while campaigning, but if elected will do whatever it takes to protect the Federal Reserve from being subjected to an audit.

Dr. Paul recognizes that the government is expanding; taxes are increasing; millions are unemployed; and hundreds of thousands of young people can't get jobs to enable them to pay on their student loans while being trapped in a bankruptcy-prison system that requires young people to pay as much as they can for 20 years instead of the normal 7 before the debt can be discharged. Dr. Paul knows that food prices are rising while Fed-created inflation is increasing; foreclosures are rising (because the government protects the banks and won't let them go bankrupt); more senseless wars are being planned in the Middle East (Iran) and our basic freedoms are disappearing. That is the "status quo" and most of the other candidates running have their own personal agendas to maintain the status quo. They just holler that they are "conservative." Being "conservative" and "status quo" are two completely different things.

The year 2008 was the first time I met Dr. Paul at one of his book signings in Austin, Texas. I had read his "The Revolution: A Manifesto"[2] and had learned from it, so I had gone to the store where the signing was taking place, to ask him to sign my copy of the book and to congratulate him on his work.

The next time I met him in Austin, I had been simply part of the large crowd that had gathered to hear him speak at the University of Texas South Mall. After the speech I had a brief chance to say hello, but to him I was simply one of tens of thousands of admirers he has met.

While Dr. Paul had been speaking that day at UT, I had memory flashbacks to 1964 when I would walk across that same mall daily on my way to engineering classes. Having just turned 21, I was about to exercise my first opportunity to vote. I knew the definition of "true conservative" and saw the personification of that concept in Senator Barry Goldwater who was campaigning against President Lyndon B. Johnson that year.

To me, a true conservative is an individual who is treated with respect by the government; one who is a forceful advocate of the U.S. Constitution and the Bill of Rights; one who is generous to others who have little in life; and one who resents government acting as the expensive "middle-man" that extorts hard earned money from the individual to satisfy collectivist notions. I knew at the time what a true

9

conservative is, because my upbringing was like the upbringing of millions of other American children who can say: "I was a 'child of the 50s.'"

I was born at the beginning of World War II, and living conditions for my family in Chicago were bleak until after the war finally ended. We returned to Texas and I entered public school. I recited the pledge of allegiance every day. I loved my country and was heavily influenced with admiration for my parent's love and loyalties to this country; and admiration for the other military veterans who were the parents of my friends who had fought a terrible war to keep fascism away. They had returned home free to build a new life in the nation we all loved.

I learned at a young age the wonder of the freedoms of private property, individual liberty and truth in America. As school children, we were taught that our government would never lie to us. We were told that it was the communist Russian and Chinese governments that lied to their people and no one wanted to be like them. Those were the days of seemingly unending "five-year economic plans" in austere Russia and China; but as a cold war escalated we had to practice ducking under our school desks and covering our heads in case the Russians decided to bomb America.

In our America of the '50s, there were no storm troopers ready to break into people's homes and arrest our father or mother, and no teams of social workers who would carry us away in the middle of the night; and no drug dealers standing on street corners or in front of convenience stores with politicians saying "Yes, someday we must do something about the 'War on Drugs'." Parents and children were not deluged 24 hours every day on television with car chases, murder and mayhem in places distant from where they lived, involving people they did not know.

Men and women were free to offer a professional service, start their own businesses, fill out very few forms, hire people to work for them and make a profit; or go bankrupt and then pick themselves up and try again. Bankers were satisfied to lend money at non-usurious rates while engaging in prudent lending practices and taking as few losses as possible—no one back then had heard of banks being "too big to fail." Insurance companies were able to offer life and medical insurance policies at nominal, competitive prices and were not forced by the government to charge the same premiums to policy holders that are charged to those people who engage in dangerous lifestyles. People paid their taxes with no thought that future politicians and U.S. Treasury officials would get away with not paying their own taxes.

People were free to explore for minerals and build necessary transmission and transportation lines; and build towns and cities and roads and bridges with very few government regulations written by federal bureaucrats who carry a treasonous hidden agenda of stopping America's development and sapping America's strength. Engineers were able to design industries, bridges, roads, water and wastewater treatment systems, with ingenuity and concern for the environment and free from a government that contended it knew better; and build dams to satisfy the thirst of the nation, and to hold back flood waters to protect people's lives and property.

But things were happening in the 1950s that slowly began the economic turmoil that the nation now endures. One of the originators of the collectivist Federal Reserve, Paul Warburg of the Council of Foreign Relations, told the U.S. Senate in 1950: "We shall have World Government, whether or not we like it. The only question is whether World Government will be achieved by conquest or consent."[3] Then by 1954, other bankers set out to form a single European currency that many years later would become known as the "euro."

President Dwight David Eisenhower appointed Earl Warren to be Chief Justice of the U.S. Supreme Court (which Eisenhower later admitted was a mistake); and many conservatives contend it was the Warren Court that began the slow decimation of our Constitution, particularly in areas of private property (nationalizing domestic oil companies by nationalizing oil pricing at the wellhead) while simultaneously gaining favor for advancing fairness in matters of race relations. During one of Eisenhower's last speeches as president, he warned the nation of the rise of the "military industrial complex."

In 1957, Ayn Rand wrote her prophetic *Atlas Shrugged*[4] novel about individuals facing off against a futuristic collectivist-American government. Then, in 1960, Senator Barry Goldwater wrote *The Conscience of a Conservative*[5] to address the rise of national collectivism

11

and the corresponding loss of individual freedoms. In 1962, the movie *The Manchurian Candidate*[6] was released, with the story ending shortly after a communist-puppet-presidential candidate had prepared to present a fiery speech to a national party convention.

Polls taken back then reflected the spirit, sense of patriotism and overall high regard that most Americans had for their country, with 70 percent believing that the government would do the right thing for the American people—a number that would drop to about 50 percent in the 1970s and down to 15 percent where it sits today in 2011.[7]

Like most other Americans, I was shocked and angered the day that President John F. Kennedy was assassinated—November 22, 1963—but simply angered when a congressional investigation in the late 1970s quietly confirmed what I had believed all along, that both President Kennedy and Dr. Martin Luther King, Jr. had been victims of conspiracies, not victims of "lone nuts" as the government and Media had worked so hard to convince us of for fifteen years. The United States government had lied to us in the same manner that communist Russia and China lied to its own people, and our faith in our own government slipped.

In 2008, voter fraud throughout the United States was rampant, and now going into 2012 there is the possibility of another stolen election. Easily-hacked or reprogrammed Diebold voting machines were used in several states to corrupt the voting process, casting doubt on the validity of election outcomes in entire states. Street thugs used intimidation tactics to keep people from voting in various precincts. During the primaries leading into both the Republican and Democratic national conventions, leaders of both the Republican and Democratic National Committees defrauded voters and delegates by breaking party rules.[8] The end result of the "hope and change" deception that took place in 2008 was the election of Barack Obama to the presidency.

Now, Mitt Romney appears to have adopted the same campaign tactics that Rick Perry used in Texas to remain governor for as long as he has. Romney no longer wants to actually debate the issues, preferring instead to give pre-scripted speeches, rely on paid advertisements and high dollar contributions from Wall Street elites, as well as rely on mainstream media support with free exposure to the nation's television viewers, and answering "softball questions" thrown at him by the supportive and protective Media. Romney's weaknesses include his many different positions on the same subject so his advisers must deemphasize his positions so that the voters won't really know what Romney stands for until he is in office—sort of like what happened to the nation when it selected Barack Obama to be president. To accomplish such a herculean task, Romney's campaign has reportedly employed over a hundred different consultants who have struggled to reformat and repackage the Romney brand away from Romney being the "moderate" Republican governor of the most liberal state in the United States, into a red-meat social conservative and heir to the Ronald Reagan legacy.[9]

Although Herman Cain describes himself as "conservative", most of the Republican candidates in the presidential race, including Cain, seem willing to do whatever it takes to prevent an audit of the private banking cartel known as the Federal Reserve. Herman Cain was a deputy chairman of the Federal Reserve in Kansas City and eventually became its chairman—which is an elitist position in banking circles. Cain recently made an unfortunate, but perhaps revealing remark that will likely undermine his chances with millions of unemployed Americans when he said: "Don't blame Wall Street, don't blame the big banks. If you don't have a job and you are not rich, blame yourself!"[10] It's doubtful that Herman Cain really understands what being "conservative" really means, by projecting his own elitist viewpoint that a "conservative" is one who lacks charity and compassion for others.

Newt Gingrich is a historian and great orator but is not a real conservative. He is a "GOP establishment's conservative" and a devoted proponent of NAFTA—the job killing trade agreement that is responsible for much of the economic hardship in the nation. He has been described as a "politician's politician" trying to be fair to all sides while trying to get reelected again. He is a fan of author Alvin Toffler's ideas for a New World Order found in two books, and Gingrich wrote the forward to one of them. Gingrich is also no Constitutional conservative, having stated in a 1995 speech to the Center for Strategic and International Affairs that "The problem for the United States in leading the world is compounded by our Constitution. Either we are going to have to rethink our Constitution or we are going to have to rethink our process of making decisions (in the United States)."[11] Gingrich has been a member of the Council of Foreign Relations[12] and has been mentored by former Secretary of State and National Security Advisor Henry Kissinger, who is also a CFR member and one-world internationalist.

And then there is New Jersey Governor Chris Christi, who has already announced that he supports Mitt Romney for President and would be interested in being the GOP vice presidential nominee. Before that statement, Kissinger had already stated that he supported Christi for president;[13] and Kissinger supports Barack Obama, also. With regard to President Obama, Kissinger has said "(Obama's) path (is) to develop an overall strategy for America in this period, when really a New World Order can be created. It's a great opportunity." Kissinger's fawning over Obama and Christi shows that there are similarities between the two that the New World Order would approve of. The New World Order is opposed to our Constitution and Christi is no true conservative.

So now the Federal Reserve, the Council on Foreign Relations, the Bilderberg Group and the New World Order all have their own candidates running for president in the next election including of course CFR-supported Barack Obama. Isn't it possible that the American people might want to have a say about who the next president will be?

Upon taking office, every President of the United States places one hand on the Bible, and then raises his (or someday her) hand and recites the following oath in accordance with Article II, Section I of the U.S. Constitution: "I do solemnly swear (or affirm) that I will faithfully execute the office of President of the United States, and will to the best of my ability, preserve, protect and defend the Constitution of the United States."

If we as a nation could elect people to high public office who took the oath of office seriously, then the nation would be much better off than it is at this time and place in its history. Defending individual liberty and the Constitution is the paramount duty of all those who seek public office; but neither President Barack Obama, former President George W. Bush, nor several other presidents who preceded those two, apparently gave any thought on Inauguration Day to that oath. Once each had spoken the words and had lowered his hand, each had found ways to pervert the meaning of the oath or ignore it altogether.

The future of the nation may well be decided in 2012. The nation is teetering on the brink of a depression and a looming major "bank-shakeout" all at the same time. We as a nation are close to becoming a slave state to a globalist financial empire that fully intends to replace our Constitution with a World Constitution crafted by the New World Order. The nation does not need any more "pretend-conservatives" or any more people like President Barack Obama in the White House.

Most definitely, the nation does not need any more presidents who represent the members of secret groups and the traitors to this nation, instead of representing all the people of the United States.

Some say that President Ronald Reagan was a true conservative, but Reagan was faced with a hostile Democratic Congress and hostile Media. After being shot and almost killed by Bush-family buddy Scott Hinckley, Jr., a physically-weakened President Reagan succumbed to the pressures placed on him by the Federal Reserve, the Media and his own vice president George H.W. Bush; and eventually did what they wanted him to do.

Before Reagan was Barry Goldwater, the true conservative. Goldwater was born in 1909 and he was an articulate speaker who served five terms as a U.S. Senator from Arizona. In 1960, Goldwater wrote about Conservatism and Individualism in his book *The Conscience of a Conservative* stating: "So it is that Conservatism, throughout history, has regarded man neither as a potential pawn of other men, nor as a part of a general collectivity in which the sacredness and the separate identity of individual human beings are ignored. Throughout history, true Conservatism has been at war equally with autocrats and with "democratic" Jacobins. The true Conservative was sympathetic with the plight of the hapless peasant under the tyranny of the French monarchy. And he was equally revolted at the attempt to solve that problem by a mob tyranny that paraded under the banner of egalitarianism. The conscience of the Conservative is pricked by anyone who would debase the dignity of the individual human being. Today, therefore, he is at odds with dictators who rule by terror, and equally with those gentler collectivists who ask our permission to play God with the human race."

Continuing, Goldwater wrote: "With this view of the nature of man, it is understandable that the Conservative looks upon politics as the art of achieving the maximum amount of freedom for individuals that is consistent with the maintenance of the social order. The Conservative is the first to understand that the practice of freedom requires the establishment of order: it is impossible for one man to be free if another is able to deny him the exercise of his freedom. But the Conservative also recognizes that the political power on which order is based is a self-aggrandizing force; that its appetite grows with eating. He knows that the utmost vigilance and care are required to keep political power within its proper bounds."

"In our day, order is pretty well taken care of. The delicate balance that ideally exists between freedom and order has long since tipped against freedom practically everywhere on earth. In some countries, freedom is altogether down and order holds absolute sway. In our country the trend is less far advanced, but it is well along and gathering momentum every day. Thus, for the American Conservative, there is no difficulty in identifying the day's overriding political challenge: it is to preserve and extend freedom. As he surveys the various attitudes and institutions and laws that currently prevail in America, many questions will occur to him, but the Conservative's first concern will always be: Are we maximizing freedom? I suggest we examine some of the critical issues facing us today with this question in mind."[14]

There appears to be nothing in the character of Rick Perry, Mitt Romney, Herman Cain, Newt Gingrich or Chris Christi that can be construed by rational Americans as being "conservative." America does not need or want President Barack Obama, nor does America need or deserve to have any of these other men serve as President of the United States. Evidence suggests their loyalties lie elsewhere.

3

The (identification) card is equipped with a VeriChip RFID tracking module which will use radio frequencies to track your every move on the planet. If this sounds foreign to you, please note that the RFID tracking chip is already in all new American passports.
~ North American Union & RFID Chip Truth

Under the Texas Constitution the governor's powers are generally limited to appointing people to serve on the states' boards and commissions and exercising the veto pen when the state legislature is in session. Under the Patriot Act, the governor can also order the Texas Department of Public Safety to spy on citizens and seize property without a warrant and ignore any form of constitutional due process.

During Rick Perry's tenure as governor, a mysterious occurrence has been taking place at a small office building located near the State Capitol in downtown Austin. On various workdays, a stocky man with sunglasses would exit the front door of the building and chain-smoke cigarettes. The man's physical appearance resembled one of John Grisham's fictional mob Morolto brothers in the movie adaptation of *The Firm.* Usually the man would stand in front of the building, smoke his cigarettes and then reenter the building.

Sometimes, after the man had been standing in front of the building for awhile, a black SUV with dark-tinted windows would pull up to the curb. A tall dark-haired man would exit the passenger side of the vehicle—also wearing sunglasses. The two men would then hustle into the building and take an elevator to a designated floor where they would then exit the elevator, walk down a hallway and enter through the door of an unmarked office.

The tall man was Governor Rick Perry who was traveling without any kind of security. There were no DPS troopers accompanying the vehicle or guarding the governor. The SUV had standard Texas license plates, not the plates issued to Texas state officials. Recently, the Republican-dominated Texas Supreme Court has ruled that Perry's travel details are secret.

Austin American Statesman reporter Jason Embry recently wrote: "As the money starts to come in, Perry's campaign organization will continue to take shape. His campaign doesn't yet have an office. Instead, a core team of Perry loyalists has run the first couple of weeks of the campaign out of one of his consultants' conference rooms near the Capitol."[15]

Those conference rooms are in the same building and are located several floors below the office that Perry had previously used and that Perry had vacated months before.

Rumors have swirled around Austin as to why the governor of Texas would have maintained a separate, private office away from the Texas Capitol Complex. One theory is that the governor was meeting secretly with wealthy supporters about state business and also his future run for president, and they had met at a location where the supporters did not have to identify themselves to a state appointment secretary or a state receptionist. Texas Open Records laws allow reporters and the public to seek public information about the governor's appointments and meetings at the state governor's office or the state Capitol, and a separate office would permit the governor to meet with people in private, without the subject matter of those meetings or even the names of the attendees ever being disclosed to reporters and the general public through formal open records requests.

Another theory is that the governor met with "backdoor" fundraisers at that building long before he announced his intention to run for president. A *New York Times* story published in the Austin American Statesman said "Before Perry even announced his candidacy, a super PAC called Americans for Rick Perry spent just under $200,000 to organize a write-in campaign on his behalf for the Ames Straw Poll in Iowa.... According to a study published by the Center for Responsive Politics, more than 80 percent of the money raised by all Republican-leaning super Pacs this year has come from just 36 donors. Democratic-leaning super PACs relied on an even smaller group, with more than 80 percent of contributions coming from just 23 donors."[16]

Another theory is that the meetings involved creation of a "Nixonian enemies list." The Richard Nixon administration had compiled a list of about 200 political opponents with another list compiled of twenty individuals listed "for special attention."[17] As described by the White House Counsel's Office, the official purpose of the list was to "screw" Nixon's political enemies by means of tax audits from the Internal Revenue Service and by manipulating "grant availability, federal contracts, litigation, prosecution, etc." In a memorandum from then-White House Counsel John Dean to White House Assistant Chief of Staff Lawrence Higby, Dean explained the purpose of the list:

> "This memorandum addresses the matter of how we can maximize the fact of our incumbency in dealing with persons known to be active in their opposition to our Administration; stated a bit more bluntly—how we can use the available federal machinery to screw our political enemies."[18]

Governor Perry has been projecting some of the same unsavory tendencies that were attributed to President Nixon. Ray Sullivan is currently communications director for Governor Rick Perry's presidential campaign. On August 28, 2011, Austin American Statesman reporter Ken Herman reported that Sullivan had called the newspaper, expressing concern about a local political activist who "is a problem for Perry."

The Herman news story indirectly disclosed that Rick Perry's associates could be keeping dossiers on any number of Texas citizens who have opposed Perry's policies as governor in the past—dossiers intended to discredit anyone with knowledge of Rick Perry's activities as governor. Herman was evidently shown only one dossier and wrote: "The Perry dossier on Morrow, shared with reporters, says he is 'an intelligent, articulate guy (Princeton degree, MBA from UT-Austin), but he has an obsessive personality…. And he has focused his obsessions on one off-the-wall political conspiracy theory after another, usually focused on alleged sexual transgressions and murder." Herman also wrote that "The Perry campaign in unflattering terms is working to discredit Morrow and discourage journalists from dealing with him. His current obsession is Texas Governor Rick Perry."[19]

There are probably many people who Governor Perry's associates have been keeping dossiers on, including probably me—not to say that I haven't earned such a status. It is well known that Governor Rick Perry hates professional engineers like me who are willing to testify as an expert witness in court on behalf of defrauded consumers who sue their homebuilders over shoddy construction practices. Many homebuilders contribute money to Mr. Perry's campaigns. One Houston homebuilder, Bob Perry who is no relation to Governor Rick Perry, is one of Perry's largest known contributors.[20]

Normally I deal with civil litigation matters; but in 2005, acting on a tip concerning possible corrupt practices taking place at the Texas Board of Professional Engineers I began looking into Governor Perry's board appointees to that particular agency. I learned a lot, including the fact that "five or six" Texas professional engineers are targeted, presumably by the Perry administration. I then contacted two members of the Texas Legislature. After those contacts, some board members and at least one agency staff employee terminated their employment or involvement with state activities.

One of Governor Perry's key goals of his version of "tort reform" has been to deny the rights of trial by jury to defrauded consumers, and more recently, to try to enact laws that would force defrauded homebuyers to pay the homebuilder's attorney's fees under a British system.

When anyone has been harmed or injured by others, under the American system of justice that person has the right to file a civil lawsuit; however, that person must also have a case that can be proven. When scientific proof is required, people with sound expertise in the applicable area of scientific practice must be retained in order to help prevent the judge and jury from exposure to "junk science" by one side or the other. I have been practicing architectural, structural and civil engineering as a licensed professional engineer for over forty years, most of that time in Texas. I have been CEO of several architectural engineering, construction-related firms. I not only conduct engineering design of the physical infrastructure, I investigate unsafe construction practices and accidents. I also help attorneys resolve civil disputes among parties in litigation as an expert engineer-witness. I sometimes am asked to appear at depositions and civil trials.

One of most important elements of establishing true scientific testimony and protecting all parties involved in a litigation matter is the acquisition and retention of key documents by the expert witness. As part of my litigation-expert witness duties, I am often provided with documents and other forms of evidence that must be protected from theft or examination by unauthorized persons. At various times, those documents include confidential and sensitive information that is provided to me by state and federal authorities. In some cases I am under a court order not to disclose certain documents or even identify my client to others.

Over a period of time I had obtained various documents and witness statements concerning the Texas engineer's board, Governor Rick Perry, and also some of his friends. For a period of time I kept those documents in my office. As the bulk of documents grew, I moved them to one of two units in a secure storage facility that I lease in Austin on behalf of my engineering firm. The documents had been placed in files next to other files and assorted evidence that I use in other litigation matters. After final conclusion of the various cases, I usually see to it that the stored documents are destroyed.

In April, 2010, my publisher released my book: *The Mysterious Adventures of Marshal Yeager, Professional Engineer – Book 1, In the Matter of: Sandra Bullock's House, Governor Rick Perry, and Corruption at the Texas Board of Professional Engineers*. I was later told that the book was widely read by members of the Texas legislature soon after it was released. The book directly or indirectly contributed to the closing of another corrupt state agency—the Texas Residential Construction Commission—an agency that had defrauded many new Texas homebuyers. The agency had been created several years before, under the pen of Governor Rick Perry, to protect some of his homebuilder contributors. I was told that at least one homebuilder-contributor was extremely angry about my book and the closure of the agency, so when I heard that I then provided some documents to the authorities.

I was out of the country in early June, 2010 traveling with my passport. On June 13, 2010, using my credit card, I checked out of my hotel and arrived at Paris–Charles DeGaulle Airport about 11:30 pm CDT. I checked my baggage and picked up my boarding pass. I purchased two chocolate truffles with euro coins at a small shop in the airport and then boarded my flight, leaving the Paris airport about 3:30 am CDT the morning of June 14, 2010.

My plane arrived at Houston's George Bush International Airport about 2:00 pm CDT the afternoon of June 14th. A customs agent asked if I was bringing any food into the country. I told the agent, "No." The agent then looked at his computer monitor and asked, "What about the chocolate truffles?" I said, "I ate them on the flight." The agent then let me pass on through. At that point in time I realized that almost everything I had spent or done, and on what date and at what time I did it, was probably on a government computer somewhere.

I was unaware at the time that all new America passports are now equipped with an RFID tracking chip to track an American's every move on the planet. Passport, travel and credit card records would indicate to government agents that I was far away from Austin on both June 13th and 14th, 2010. Without my knowledge at the time, on June 13th or 14th both storage units were entered by persons unknown.

I spent the night of June 14, 2010, in a Houston hotel, checking in using a credit card about 3:30 pm. I left Houston very early by car and arrived back in Austin the morning of June 15, 2010. On the morning of June 16, 2010, I visited the storage facility. There are hundreds of storage units in the facility. The facility is surrounded by a tall, security fence. The facility maintains 24-hour on-site management. There are management living quarters and an office located within the fenced area. The entry gate to the facility requires an electronic code. The only other entry from outside the fence leading into the facility is through the management office.

One of my engineering firm's storage units is located off a hallway within an air-conditioned, free standing building that is located near the management office. Another storage unit is simply part of a row of non-air-conditioned units that are located outside the air conditioned facility at a location that faces the management office. The doors to both units are locked with expensive, high grade padlocks that I had purchased from the facility management.

When I approached the exterior door of the air-conditioned building the morning of June 16th, I realized that the door leading into the building was unsecured. The door was steel but the combination lock that had been mounted within the door itself was missing. The combination lock was the first line of defense against an unauthorized intrusion into any of the storage units within the building. I simply pulled open the door and walked into the hallway.

The hallway leads past several other storage units to the locked door of my firm's storage unit. I commonly utilize a method to determine if someone has entered the unit without my permission. Upon inspecting the door and lock, unlocking the lock and then opening the door, I realized that the unit had been entered in my absence. Checking the exterior, non-air-conditioned storage unit, I saw that it had been entered as well.

I asked the facility manager what had happened to the combination lock that had been mounted into the steel door leading into the air-conditioned building. The manager stated that they were replacing the door and that the combination lock had been removed so that a new door could be installed. I stated that anyone could easily access the hallway from the exterior with the combination lock removed. I then asked when the combination lock had been removed. The manager replied "two or three" days ago. That would indicate the lock was removed on June 13th or June 14th exposing the inside storage unit to an intruder, about the time I was returning to the United States.

I reported the incident to the police on June 17, 2010, and then met with a police officer at the scene. That same day I saw that a

23

combination lock trim plate had since been installed on what appeared to be the same door, but the combination lock itself was still missing.

The padlocks had not been damaged or scratched. According to the manager, and confirmed by another individual who arrived in the office at the same time that the police officer and I were present, there was no master key to the padlocks. The management company uses bolt cutters to remove the locks whenever they need to clean out a unit for failure to pay rent.

I asked the manager if their computers were firewalled and was told that the computers had been upgraded "about four months ago" making it highly unlikely that a person could have determined from the Internet which particular storage units had been leased by my engineering firm. Upon my further questioning, the manager stated that no search warrant had been shown to her to allow someone to inspect any of the units leased by my firm; however, the manager refused to answer if anyone had approached her about entering the units.

I had the only keys to the padlocks for each storage unit, and no one but me knew the exact location of the units or even where the storage facility was located in Austin. It was becoming evident that the existence of the storage units, and their location, could have been obtained only from bank records by a high government official using the Patriot Act.

The exterior steel door with the combination lock at issue was the one facing the 24 hour living quarters and office. The building is large and there are two other access doors that are out of view of the manger's living quarters and office. I wondered why someone would choose to break into a combination lock that faced the living quarters and office, instead of entering through one of the other doors out of sight of the office.

When I returned to the facility on June 25, 2010, I discovered that a combination lock had been installed in the exterior door. The combination lock appeared to be new. I inspected the door, and the door was the same old door that had been there before. I recalled the threshold weather sweep had been previously bent, and the sweep was still bent. This could indicate that the lock was not "removed so that a new door could be installed", and that the manager had been most likely lying.

Management claimed that there were no security cameras on the property, which I found unusual in this post-9/11 world. The only cameras I could see were located nearby at a major traffic intersection with one camera pointed toward the road in front of the facility.

Under the Patriot Act, a senior government official, including a state governor, can order law enforcement to search the property of any American citizen without a search warrant and without the citizen knowing about it. If state or federal agents had ordered my banker to disclose the location of the storage facility, he would have had to follow their orders; but if he were to tell me about it he could go to jail.

The same is true for the storage facility manager. Using the Patriot Act, a single government agent could have demanded access to the storage units without obtaining or showing a search warrant. The agent could have then had a locksmith remove the padlocks to the doors of both units, leaving no trace that the locks and doors had been opened. If a government agent had ordered the manager to damage and remove the combination lock at the front of the building to make it appear that a burglar had damaged the lock, in case I did discover the intrusions, and the manager had later told me the truth—that the agent had issued the order—then under the Patriot Act the manager could also go to jail.

A detailed check of the contents of both units revealed that nothing was missing from either unit. Several weeks before I had gone overseas, I had moved all of the files pertaining to the Texas engineering board, including those of Governor Rick Perry and his friends, to another location untraceable through bank records. When I checked that location, I saw that the documents had not been disturbed.

Next I was subjected to additional state-sanctioned harassment. The official purpose of President Nixon's enemies list was to "screw" Nixon's political enemies by means of tax audits from the Internal Revenue Service, and Governor Rick Perry appears to have taken a part of that historical playbook to heart. Although the IRS ignored

Nixon's bid to audit the people who had been placed on the list, Texas Comptroller Susan Combs, who heads the Texas tax authority, appears to have followed Nixon's lead.

Comptroller Combs' tenure as Texas Comptroller has been fraught with mismanagement. According to the Austin American Statesman, in April 2010 "thousands of consumers seeking rebates for energy-efficient appliances could not get access through phone banks or a website." That incident occurred about the time that the Comptroller, in violation of the Texas Constitution, was refusing to provide an update on the then-suspected, now confirmed state budget crisis. Governor Perry had been facing two strong opponents in the Texas Republican primary at the time, and any hint of state financial problems or impropriety could have potentially sunk Perry's reelection chances as governor. Comptroller Combs waited until after Governor Perry's successful re-election before presenting the bad news about the state budget to the citizens of Texas.

On January 10, 2011, my company received a Texas Workforce Commission notice-of-audit to be conducted on February 2, 2011. The audit was initially to include individual payroll information; general ledgers, chart of accounts and disbursement journals, payroll journals and time cards, all cancelled checks and check stubs, quarterly reports, current ownership forms, profit and loss statements, master vendor files, and corporate charter and minutes. Then, on January 22nd, a state agent called the company CPA requesting copies of IRS forms W-2, W-3, 1096, 1099, 940 and 941; plus copies of company bank statements, check registers, IRS tax return, and copies of employee paychecks.

The audit was eventually completed on February 9, 2011, and it wound up serving as an example of state harassment of my small business. I wound up paying a total of $15 to the state due to a delayed-payment penalty and also paid a large amount of money to the company CPA who had to deal with the issue. It was the first time that my Texas engineering firm had been audited in its 23-year history by the Texas Workforce Commission, but a greater surprise was yet to come.

On April 12, 2011 the Austin American-Statesman reported that personal and confidential data of 3.5 million Texans receiving unemployment checks had been left exposed to the Internet by Comptroller Combs for about a year. Also left unprotected were the personal records of teachers, state workers, retirees, and practically everyone else employed by a public or private employer in Texas. Left exposed to anyone who wanted to look, were Social Security numbers, addresses, dates of birth, wages, and more, on millions of Texas citizens.

The Statesman article quoted Jason Lavender of ID Theft Solutions of America who said it is potentially "a very big deal for the people who are affected," noting that the case opens the door for a number of different types of identity theft, not just financial, and that Social Security numbers and birth dates can be sold to illegal immigrants."

Personnel with the Texas Comptroller's office had placed the information on a publicly accessible server where it was available from the Internet for about one year. The privacy violation was reportedly fixed on March 31, 2011 six weeks after my company's accounts had been audited by the Texas Workforce Commission, which is the same agency that then undoubtedly uploaded the information to the Internet and to the Office of the Comptroller led by Susan Combs.

According to the Statesman article, the vulnerable data originated with the Texas Workforce Commission, plus the Teacher Retirement System, the Employees Retirement System, and the Department of Public Safety. Those four agencies collect personal information, including wages, on practically everyone in the state. The law requires the information to be reported to the Comptroller. Reuters noted that "the Texas Workforce Commission data breach was the most widespread, containing records of some 2 million individuals."

People who work for a private employer in Texas probably know that their employer is required to report their wages to the Texas Workforce Commission. Employers who have had their business accounts audited by TWC are vulnerable to disclosure of critical business information, including payments to and receipts from, confidential customers and clients who demand a fiduciary duty of protection. The Texas attorney general and FBI have opened a criminal investigation, according to Jerry Strickland, a spokesman for Attorney General Greg Abbot.

All American citizens are now vulnerable to spying by state and federal government officials and violations of due process, including search and seizure without a warrant under the Patriot Act. Under Governor Rick Perry, millions of Texas citizens and Texas businesses have also had their personal and financial privacy violated as well.

4

∽ EDUCATION, JOBS, AND A KICKBACK
TO THE WEALTHY ∾

The other purpose of taxation, according to Ruml, is to redistribute the wealth from one class of citizens to another. This must always be done in the name of social justice or equality, but the real objective is to override the free market and bring society under the control of the master planners.
~ G. Edward Griffin, "The Creature from Jekyll Island: A Second Look at the Federal Reserve"

It is fair to say that Governor Rick Perry has been a driving force behind the economic and social policies implemented in Texas over the past decade, and by a wide range of benchmarks, Texas is worse off now than it was when Governor Perry took office from former Governor George W. Bush.

In 2003 Governor Perry called three consecutive special legislative sessions in order to procure a congressional redistricting plan that enabled more Republicans than Democrats to get elected. The redistricting plan that was finally adopted, supported by then U.S. House Majority Leader Tom DeLay, brought about a five-seat Republican gain in the Texas delegation. As a result, for all practical purposes, Texas Democrats have been out of power for a decade.

According to Take Back Texas Alliance,[21] Texas has the highest percentage of citizens without health insurance among all 50 states. This lack of insurance coverage places additional stress on hospital emergency rooms and other health care facilities of last resort. Texas ranks 50th nationally in Medicaid reimbursement rates, and the state ranks 42nd in the nation in taxes and fees collected as a percentage of personal income.

College tuition rates in Texas used to be among the lowest in the nation, but this is no longer true. With the reduction of state funding for higher education and the deregulation of college tuition in 2003, college tuition rates have increased dramatically over the past eight years. This past decade the State of Texas has covered less and less of the cost of public education, with local property taxes funding an increasing share of the state's responsibility.

After the legislative adoption of significant insurance deregulation in 2003, Texas homeowners' insurance rates then soared. Texans now pay the highest homeowners' insurance rates in the nation.

Texas ranks 11th nationally in local property taxes, and that ranking is almost certain to rise with the reduction in state funding for public education and the pressure to raise local property taxes once again.

The exorbitant homeowners' insurance rates and local property taxes act as a heavy burden on the most valuable assets that many Texans own—their homes. The middle class in Texas has suffered mightily during the past ten years, and the state budget cuts will unquestionably eliminate thousands of jobs, cause unemployment to rise, and reduce gross state income. This is not the kind of future that is good for the people of Texas, and adopting such policies for our nation would be even worse.

Contrary to political rhetoric, Governor Rick Perry does not have a great reputation for improving education and creating jobs in Texas. According to the Take Back Texas Alliance, Mr. Perry's policies have "done enormous harm to schoolchildren, the disabled, the young and the poor in Texas." By the end of 2011, Texas will be either last or close to last in a large number of categories that measure the state's investment in the future. Two of the most critical benchmarks are public and higher education.

The tide of public pressure against the public school budget cuts began mounting in early 2011. Thousands of concerned Texans turned out for two rallies at the State Capitol on March 12th and 14th, to protest proposed cuts to public education. Legislators from both parties acknowledged that they were receiving intense constituent pressure in opposition to the proposed cuts.

Nevertheless, during the recent, 82nd legislative session, the Texas legislature enacted a measure that intentionally violates an 1876 provision of the Texas Constitution. The 1876 provision had required the state of Texas to provide adequate funding for public schools:

Article 7: "A general diffusion of knowledge being essential to the preservation of the liberties and rights of the people, it shall be the duty of the Legislature of the State to establish and make suitable provision for the support and maintenance of an efficient system of public free schools."

The 82nd Legislature repealed a 1949 legislative compact guaranteeing a funding formula for public education. The legislature can now appropriate whatever level of funding it considers appropriate for public education. To do this, the state now pretends that Texas public schools have no new students for funding purposes. Unless this new law is changed, it will remain in effect during the 83rd Legislative Session that will convene in January 2013.

According to Take Back Texas Alliance, ten years ago Texas ranked 25th nationally in spending per capita for Texas public schools. Today, the state ranks 46th nationally, and after the budget cuts for public education are fully implemented in September 2011, Texas will be last in the nation in per capita spending for public education. Texas is number 1 in the nation in the growth of child poverty, and now Texas has the lowest percentage in the nation of residents over 25 with a high school diploma.

With regard to higher education, the University of Texas experienced a 16% cut in its budget, Texas A&M University a 13% cut, and Southwestern Medical School in Dallas a 22% cut. The University of Texas now receives approximately 13% of its total funding from the State of Texas and is essentially turning into a semi-private university highly dependent on donations and other sources of funding as a result of the increasingly draconian funding levels that have been appropriated by the state legislatures in recent years.

31

The projections indicate that tens of thousands of teachers and school personnel will be laid off due to the budget cuts, and many thousands of additional public and private Texas jobs will also be lost as a result.

Texas, tied for first with Mississippi in the overall percentage of minimum wage jobs, is fast becoming a banana republic, with an enormous gap between rich and poor and a regressive and antiquated tax code that is incapable of generating enough revenue to provide even the most rudimentary state services for the Texas population. Projections indicate that if present trends continue, much of the state economy will suffer in the future with a poorly educated population that will attract only those industries that offer minimum wage jobs.

According to Take Back Texas Alliance, the roots of Texas' current budget crisis arose from a state law proposed in 2006. At that time, Governor Rick Perry proposed that a "tax swap" be enacted through a new "margins tax" in response to a Texas Supreme Court ruling that an unconstitutional statewide property tax was in effect. The ruling was based on the fact that most local school district property taxes were at the maximum $1.50 cap allowed by state law.

Governor Perry's proposal called for substantial state revenue reductions in property taxes in exchange for equivalent revenue increases generated by the so-called "margins tax" on Texas businesses based on a "tax swap." On May 15, 2006, then-State Comptroller Carole Keeton Strayhorn wrote a letter to Governor Perry, warning Perry and the Legislature that the "tax swap" was "$23 billion short of the funds that were needed to pay for the promised property tax cuts over the next five years." Since that time, Comptroller Strayhorn's projections have been verified by the facts. The margins tax became law when Governor Perry signed the bill, and is now the root cause of the astounding record $26.9 billion deficit that Texas faces for the upcoming 2012-2013 biennium.

Ms. Strayhorn had projected that the "structural deficits" for 2009 and 2010 would total $9.9 billion. On January 31, 2011, the State Comptroller's Office testified before the Senate Finance Committee that the structural deficit was currently $10 billion. In her letter, Ms. Strayhorn had stated: "At worst, it will relegate Texans to draconian cuts in critical areas like education and health care for at least a generation." This description accurately describes the budget cuts adopted by the Texas House in its budget (House Bill 1) approved on April 3, 2011.

Governor Perry convinced state legislators that Comptroller Strayhorn was attacking the margins tax purely for political reasons, since she was running for governor as an independent at the time. The margins tax was also extremely complex, and very few people understood it. This complexity enabled Governor Perry to misrepresent it, and ultimately was a major factor behind the Legislature's decision to approve it. Ultimately, large corporate homebuilders and other contributors to Governor Perry benefitted from the very large loopholes that the margins tax provided.

The margins tax is unique to Texas and has not been adopted by any other state, most likely because of the disaster it has now wrought on the Texas budget. In an article titled "NFIB calls Texas' business margin tax a "lose-lose' situation",[22] writer Paul Wiseman states, "In the 2007 session the Texas Legislature enacted a 'margin' tax on businesses, a levy that was expected to raise significant revenue for state coffers. Instead, many have pointed out this tax has fallen short of projections by more than $2 billion in each of the last two years. On the other hand it has greatly raised both taxes and peripheral expenses on many small businesses, according to Laura Hoke of the Texas chapter of the National Federation of Independent Businesses."

"We look at the tax as an abject failure," said Hoke, "because it's crippling the small and mid-sized businesses without bringing in what (the legislators) thought. It's a lose-lose scenario." The NFIB would prefer the state to return to the franchise tax law, which the margins levy replaced, wherein a company was taxed on profits, not on gross income.

Hoke made reference to one trucking company whose franchise tax burden had been approximately $6,000 per year, but whose numbers under the margin structure skyrocketed to $60,000. While that is an extreme case, it is not isolated. And although some have had increases of only $200 or so, "Most companies have seen a 100-500 percent increase," she reported.

Hidden in the strain on business finances is the cost of compliance. Hoke told of an engineering firm that had been paying its CPA $1,500 to calculate its taxes under the old system. To calculate the new version, the company was being billed $4,500. All those costs restrict a business's ability to hire, increase inventory or otherwise grow itself and contribute to the state's economy, she noted.

According to State Representative Mike Villarreal, D-San Antonio, who is widely considered to be the preeminent budget expert in the Texas House, Texas has a total of 227 tax exemptions, exclusions and discounts in its tax code that total $66 billion in tax loopholes for 2012/2013. That is $66 billion that cannot be collected in taxes from several of Governor Rick Perry's contributors benefitting from the margins tax. The elimination of $27 billion of these tax loopholes would have caused the deficit to disappear, and the spending cuts that will cause so much needless suffering and economic harm to Texas would have never been adopted.

The Texas Tax Code is broken and is not producing sufficient revenue to meet the most basic needs of the state. The special interests, many of whom have supported Governor Perry, benefit from the tax loopholes at the expense of the entire state.

Democrat John Sharp, working in alliance with Governor Perry, is said to have played a major role in the development of the margins tax law. Sharp chaired the committee that proposed the tax. Governor Perry, through his appointed regents who also have contributed a lot of money to Perry's campaigns, has recently awarded Sharp the chancellorship of Texas A&M University. Perry had previously appointed his chief of staff, Mike McKinney, to be the chancellor at Texas A&M. McKinney was under pressure from Perry's regents who felt he was not assertive enough in pursuing controversial changes in a higher education policy championed by Governor Perry and another major Perry donor, Jeff Sandefer.[23] Perry and McKinney were rumored to have had once been close, but Perry ruthlessly forced McKinney out. Governor Perry then appointed Sharp to the position at Texas A&M. At one point in time, it was assumed that John Sharp would run for the U.S. Senate to fill Senator Kay Bailey Hutchison's seat.

According to *AOL Daily Finance*,[24] Texas has two cities with the worst poverty rate in the nation. El Paso has over 41,000 poor, with a city poverty rate of 24.3 percent and a suburban poverty rate of 31 percent. McAllen, Texas has over 217,000 poor, with a city poverty rate of 28.3 percent and a suburban poverty rate of 36.7 percent.

El Paso is located on the Rio Grande along the U.S.–Mexico border, across from Cuidad Juarez. It is home to branches of a number of large manufacturers, including Boeing, Hoover, Eureka and Delphi. Yet, according to AOL, El Paso had an extremely high overall poverty rate of 23.7 percent in 2009. This compares to Texas's overall rate of 17.1 percent in the same year. El Paso's economic situation has improved somewhat with the recent expansion of Ft. Bliss, which is now one of the largest military bases in the country; however, unemployment remains at 10.9 percent which is almost 17 percent higher than the national average.

McAllen is another boarder town based along the Rio Grande at the southern tip of Texas. More than 85% of McAllen's poor live in the suburbs outside of the city. According to Brookings, as of 2009, 35.4 percent of McAllen's suburban poor are born outside of the U.S. reflecting a huge number of people who have crossed the southern border into the United States and have stayed in Texas. The metropolitan area's economy has grown rapidly in the last few years due to job growth in government, education and health care; however, in June 2011, unemployment increased to 13 percent, up from 11.9 percent the month before. According to AOL, the city has the lowest median household income in the nation.

Texas faces the financial apocalypse that Ms. Strayhorn predicted. The stakes have never been higher. Texas must have sufficient additional revenues to eliminate the need for budget cuts. The Texas legislature did not fix the permanent hole in the budget (the structural deficit) with additional revenues this legislative session, and the hole will more than double again in two years regardless of how the economy performs.

What Governor Perry misrepresented to the people of Texas was a tax "cut" for certain large corporations, disguised as a tax "swap," and many of the ultimate beneficiaries were Governor Rick Perry's millionaire-billionaire friends. Had Perry admitted that the "tax swap" was actually a "tax cut" in 2006, the disastrous effects of this change would have been widely acknowledged, and the margins tax probably would never have been enacted into law.

The fiscal deception created by Governor Perry has produced a permanent hole in the Texas state budget and created the enormous budget deficit that Governor Perry and his allies then used to justify the draconian budget cuts that were enacted by the Texas Legislature. As Rep. Villarreal's analysis shows, the permanent hole in the Texas budget will continue to grow and cause widespread harm to the state's economy as well as the state's future.

5

ᕱ WEIRD WIZARDS AND TALK OF TREASON ᕬ

A nation can survive its fools and even the ambitious. But it cannot survive treason from within. An enemy at the gates is less formidable, for he is known and he carries his banners openly against the city. But the traitor moves among those within the gates freely. His sly whispers rustling through all the alleys, heard in the very halls of government itself. For the traitor appears no traitor; he speaks in the accents familiar to his victims, and he wears their face and their garments and he appeals to the baseness that lies deep in the hearts of all men.

~ Cicero, speech to the Roman Senate

On August 17, 2011, only a few days after the results of the Iowa Straw Poll had been announced, newspaper headlines blared nationwide that newly-announced presidential candidate Governor Rick Perry had suggested that the Federal Reserve would come close to committing treason by deciding to print more money. According to the Austin American Statesman,[25] Governor Perry was referring to Federal Reserve Chairman Ben Bernanke when he said:

"If this guy prints more money between now and the election, I don't know what y'all would do to him in Iowa, but we would treat him pretty ugly down in Texas. Printing more money to play politics at this particular time in American history is almost treacherous, or treasonous, in my opinion."

Obama White House press secretary Jay Carney chastised Perry, saying "When you're president or you're running for president, you have to think about what you're saying, because your words have greater impact. And President Obama and we take the independence of the Federal Reserve quite seriously, and certainly think threatening the Fed chairman is probably not a good idea."

Karl Rove, a top aide in former president George W. Bush grumbled: "You don't accuse the Chairman of the Federal Reserve of being a traitor to his country. Of being guilty of treason." Then *The Washington Times*[26] wrote: "Karl Rove suggested (the Perry remarks) were a 'bid to establish distance between Mr. Perry and his former boss (then-Texas Governor George W. Bush)'. Tea Party activists and former high-ranking party officials alike see Mr. Rove and other elements in the GOP establishment increasingly fearful over what they now regard as a serious threat that Mr. Perry can take the nomination."

Former Massachusetts governor Mitt Romney said "We need to recognize we need to have a Fed; while former Kansas City Federal Reserve Chairman Herman Cain said, "I don't believe in ending the Fed. I believe in fixing the Fed." Cain made his comment after he had flippantly denied the need to audit the Federal Reserve at all.

While hosting the December 29, 1010 Neil Boortz Radio Show, Mr. Cain had said: "Some people say that we ought to audit the Federal Reserve.... Now I no longer serve on the board of the Federal Reserve.... Call them up, and ask them if you can stop by and have one of their PR people or one of their public relations people explain to you how the Federal Reserve operates. I think a lot of people are calling for this audit of the Federal Reserve because they don't know enough about it. There's no hidden secrets going on in the Federal Reserve to my knowledge.... We don't need to waste money with another commission or an audit that's not necessary, because folks, we got a lot of other problems we need to worry about."

Later *The Washington Times* opined:[27]

"Recently, in Iowa Mr. Perry said that Federal Reserve Chairman Ben Bernanke's 'quantitative easing'—massively printing money—is 'almost treasonous,' especially, if he was

38

to unleash the printing presses for a third round in order to artificially boost economic growth. Apparently, for many pundits, this comment is beyond the pale. Even Great Society Republicans are upset. They argue Mr. Bernanke has been unfairly attacked, the political independence of the Federal Reserve is under assault and Mr. Perry should apologize.

"But the Texas governor is right. Mr. Bernanke's loose monetary policy is slowly eroding the dollar. A nation's economy is only as strong as its currency. The more greenbacks printed, the lower their value. The falling dollar is undermining consumer purchasing power, reducing our standard of living and inevitably leading to inflation—the great threat to middle-class prosperity. Mr. Bernanke's actions are reckless and pose a clear and present danger to America's economic security. It may not be 'treasonous' but it's darn close."

Upon hearing the word "treason" associated with the Federal Reserve, the American people were supposed to be shocked by the remarks. Shocked! But none of the critics seemed aware that, many years ago, President Harry Truman had said pretty much the same thing about the Chairman of the Federal Reserve. Truman, himself, had recognized the danger inherent in the existence of the Federal Reserve and had called the Federal Reserve Chairman a "traitor" to his face. Those were the days before "politically-correct" and controlled speech had become commonplace in America.

So what is the reason for such an outspoken reaction? Is presidential-candidate U. S. Representative Ron Paul's well-known effort to audit the Federal Reserve finally gaining traction with the voters? It certainly appears to have gained traction with the tea-party movement.

Who are the real protectors of the Federal Reserve? Could it be both President Obama and former president George W. Bush? Is it the presidents' spokespeople? The U.S. Congress? The U.S. Supreme

Court? The news media? All of the above? Or does Governor Perry believe that simply criticizing the Federal Reserve will attract the Tea Party voters to his candidacy, without Perry even realizing what he has said?

In modern American culture, the phrase "speaking of the devil" is used as a reference to someone who has just entered the room while being spoken about. In earlier days children would hear their mothers or grandmothers say "Don't speak of the Devil." The phrase enshrined the notion that it was dangerous to mention the Devil by name, lest he suddenly appear and do evil. In some cultures, the phrase translates to "Speak of the Devil and there he is." The phrase "Speak of the Devil and he will appear" originated in England where it was, and still is, more often given as "talk of the Devil."[28]

British author J. K Rowling is best known as the creator of the Harry Potter fantasy book series. The books have also become the basis for a popular series of films. In "Harry Potter and the Sorcerer's Stone," Rowling introduces her evil Lord Voldemort character as the one "who must not be named" with the lines: "We do not speak his name.... He who must not be named did great things. Terrible, yes, but great."[29]

In America, there is a force that must not be named or spoken of in an irreverent manner by persons who strive to be elevated to a higher position in life, such as President of the United States. That force is the private banking cartel known as the Federal Reserve—an entity with tremendous powers—and an evil entity at that.

Americans are wondering why they are having such a hard time, with the economy the way it is. Many are facing bankruptcy or foreclosure with seemingly no way out. Many are financially tethered to their mortgaged houses that cannot be sold—keeping the debtors from moving elsewhere. Many have lost their jobs and don't know where to turn. Many are worried about the future of their children and their grandchildren. Many complain that illegal immigrants have taken away their jobs even while states like Texas maintain "sanctuary cities" and provide college grants so that illegal immigrants can attend college.

It is important that those Americans hold on to what they've got that is meaningful to them—family, friends, community, church, pets, whatever makes them happy, and pray. Americans don't have to take it and don't need to play the game that's already been rigged against them. Americans should learn about and vote out the parasites that benefit from politically-correct speech; hyphenated race division, lawlessness, news media propaganda, the New World Order, the North American Union, NAFTA, globalism and intense regulation of their lives; and those rascals who have brought this great nation to such a low ebb.

Writer Jubal E. Harshal, expressing his opinion on an article titled "Demagoguing the Mosque and Islam"[30] wrote (edited):

"Americans need wake up; America is being invaded, and not just by Muslims. Whereas the Muslims are purposeful in their task, and are sending a message worldwide in building the Mosque in that location, the greater percentage of our invaders are primarily coming across our borders in order to share in, and export our economic wealth, with little to no loyalty to American ideals. How many realize those multimillions will be among us when the lights go fully out on our economy?

"We need awaken too, to the fact that our national leaders (traitors really) are facilitating all of the above in the name of globalism. Being a student of pre-Columbian History, I have news for our leaders. Men have been trading globally, even with the American continent, since the dawn of man. No monopolistic free trade agreements were necessary— men trade as naturally as they breathe, even across oceans in seemingly flimsy ancient vessels. How many have recognized they are now citizens of the North American Union? Indeed we are, Americans, Canadians and Mexicans, since March 2005."

Thirty years ago, in the early 1980's, many Texans were only starting to go through the suffering that many Americans are going through right now—the beginning of ten years of economic devastation and deprivation; broken families; no jobs, miles of housing subdivisions and buildings sitting vacant; and the homeless walking the streets everywhere. Even many of those who were lucky enough to find a job had to sign a three-month contract with no certainty of that the job would be extended. Other American oil-resource-states went through it too, as did the farm-belt states.

Most Texans survived and learned from the experience. Some did not survive—caught in an unspoken colonial war foisted on them by their government—dying without knowing really what had happened to them. But what had happened to them was not their fault any more than it is the fault of Americans in trouble right now.

At the time, the creditors, the media, the government and the political elite used Texas citizens' sense of honor and shame to try to make them feel like it was their own fault. After all, if everyone had just chucked it and moved away, a lot of the mooching political elite would have found themselves in financial trouble. That's why they cheat in this game of life. They believe the American people are supposed to be working to support them!

Many Texans have learned to associate Governor Rick Perry with international globalism and the Bilderberg Group. On June 7, 2007, Austin radio talk show host, Alex Jones led a group of Austin-area activists in a protest against Gov. Perry's June 2, 2007 trip to Istanbul, Turkey. Perry had attended the clandestine Bilderberg Group meeting, where world leaders, international bankers, policy-makers, global royalty, and other shadowy individuals meet annually under secret auspices. The Bilderberg Group is famous for making decisions that affect world policies. A YouTube video featuring Alex Jones protesting Perry's actions can be found referenced.[31]

In a speech, Jones discussed the New World Order seeking to control and manage all of humanity, and how regular people need to wake up and be aware of what is going on. He mentions certain powerful families such as the Rockefellers, the Rothschilds, and the George Bushes of Texas. That video can also be found in the references.[32]

Perry returned from meeting with the Bilderberg Group reportedly with a wad of money intended for the National Republican

Governor's Association, of which he has served as chairman. Suggestions were made at the time that Gov. Perry might have been in violation of the Logan Act, which forbids private correspondence and business dealings with foreign governments.

President Obama has voiced confidence that he can defeat both Rick Perry and Michele Bachmann in the election of 2012. With regard to Ron Paul, Obama has said very little. According to an early Rasmussen poll, Barack Obama and Ron Paul were virtually dead-even in a hypothetical 2012 election matchup.[33] In a more recent poll comparing Barack Obama against the entire field of Republican candidates, Obama had the lowest poll numbers while competing against Ron Paul,[34] most likely an indicator of Democrats who may be considering switching political parties to vote for Paul.

Considering Governor Rick Perry's rapid rise in the polls in such a short period of time, there are most likely powerful corporate and international financial forces at work behind his candidacy. Perry has previously shown signs of succumbing to the wishes of those who contribute large sums of money to his campaigns, throughout most of his tenure as governor of Texas. President Obama would know this, but he also probably knows that if Rick Perry tones down the rhetoric about the Federal Reserve, then Perry will most likely be able to drain money from the establishment Republican donors who are dependent on banking largesse, and gain the Republican presidential nomination in 2012.

President Obama probably already knows a great deal more about Rick Perry than does the general public. Obama's final comment about Perry's "treason" remark was "but I'll cut him some slack. He's only been at it for a few days now." Thus, President Obama might consider Perry a beatable foe if he is nominated by the Republicans.

In a recent newspaper article about 9/11, young central Texas "Millennials" were reflecting on what it was like growing up with the War on Terror. The article noted that today's young adults—the children of 9/11—will shape the nation's future. Mentioned in the article was University of Texas student Audrey White, 20, who "processed the news of Osama bin Laden's death in much the same way she processed the death of the other figure of evil—this one fictional—she had grown up with. (It had been) Lord Voldemort of the 'Harry Potter' book series. 'It was a satisfying sort of catharsis, but when the buzz faded, I looked around to find nothing about my real life had changed,' said White who was 10 in 2001."[35]

White continued: "Osama bin Laden was our real-life Voldemort, this big scary idea and this face of all the evil in the world. In the same way that we grew up with Harry Potter and Voldermort, we grew up with this scary, nebulous, hidden being with a network of evil followers who walked among us. He was the ultimate scapegoat and puppet in the agenda against terror."

Bin Laden is dead but the evil continues. For America, the ultimate puppeteer is still the one "who must not be named," especially by those who expect to get plenty of money to finance their campaigns to become members of Congress or President of the United States. That puppeteer is the Federal Reserve, and soon young voters whose entire future is at stake will figure that out.

6

✑ THE NATIONAL ECONOMY AND THE FED'S INSIDER TRADING APPARATUS ✑

Information about plans by the Federal Reserve to change interest rates could be turned into huge profits if it were known before the policy was made public…. Similar activities at private sector corporations would be treated as crimes.
~ Robert D. Auerbach, economist
U.S. House of Representatives

Presidential-candidate Rick Perry has no known education in the economic principles that underlie free enterprise and form the underpinnings of individual liberties. Like President Obama, Perry has never held an adult job in the private sector or run a business or engaged in a profession. Some in Texas say he has no real philosophy, no real virtues, and will do or say whatever it takes to get elected; and once in office he will do or say whatever he is told to do or say, in order to stay elected.

The next President of the United States will need to have a sound understanding of the financial forces that have brought this nation to where it is today, and not be simply a politician looking out for his or her own personal interests. The next President will need to be a real leader—an honest person—a person trusted to go to Washington with a soundly educated and experienced team that is capable of restoring basic American principles and the nation's financial health. The next President must not subject the American people to more finger pointing of blame, such as: "Why it couldn't possibly be Obama's

45

fault. It's Bush's fault or the Tea Party's fault or the Japanese Tsunami's fault or the weather's fault or the ATM's fault ... but certainly not Obama's fault (eye roll)."[36]

The same is true for members of the next Congress, and the next Congress after that, and subsequent Congresses until the nation's problems are solved. Future presidents and members of Congress must be elected based on their knowledge and willingness to audit the Federal Reserve to find out where the taxpayer's money went, and then return the money to those Americans whose assets were stolen; as well as to the U.S. Treasury, while simultaneously abolishing the Federal Reserve.

Fundamental to this knowledge is a sound understanding of how the Federal Reserve was able to seize the U.S. Treasury and take taxpayer dollars to support its own criminal, insider-trading enterprise.

According to the Securities and Exchange Commission, "Insider trading" is a term that most investors have heard and usually associate with illegal conduct. But the term actually includes both legal and illegal conduct. The legal version is when corporate insiders—officers, directors, and employees—buy and sell stock in their own companies. When corporate insiders trade in their own securities, they must report their trades to the SEC. Illegal insider trading refers generally to buying or selling a security, in breach of a fiduciary duty or other relationship of trust and confidence, while being in possession of material, nonpublic information about the security. Insider trading violations may also include "tipping" such information; securities trading by the person "tipped;" and securities trading by those who misappropriate such information.

No record has been found of a civil or criminal court ever applying insider trading laws to the Federal Reserve, which could partially explain why the Federal Reserve depends on so much secrecy—it will not turn over information and investigators do not know what to look for.

In 1987, Mr. William Greider wrote a book titled *Secrets of the Temple: How the Federal Reserve Runs the Country*. Mr. Greider was a former assistant managing editor for *The Washington Post* who interviewed then-Federal Reserve Chairman Paul Volcker and then-

FDIC Chairman William M. Isaac. Greider wrote about the Second Bank of the United States that was the nation's central bank until 1832:[37]

"The Second Bank of the United States, as a central bank, was descended from kings, the inheritor of the monarch's authority, and the proximate model was the Bank of England, chartered in 1694. In the United States, however, the people themselves were supposed to be the sovereign. The Second BUS accumulated enormous financial power, held the federal government's deposits interest free and was also the largest store of private wealth. It became the dominant player in foreign exchange and the domestic money market. It was the lender of last resort that could save a foundering bank or doom it. It also attempted to regulate the economy, restraining credit when it appeared that speculative lending was becoming excessive. The bank was directed by Nicholas Biddle, who became the reincarnation of autocratic control—the few ruling over the many—precisely what sincere republicans sought to escape in America.

"President Andrew Jackson's constituency was alive to opportunity—opening the frontier territory to agriculture and mining, developing roads and canals and railroads that would link up markets, constructing new towns and cities. But they felt threatened, their aspirations, their economic independence seemed endangered by an encroaching web of concentrated power—the influence of wealth represented by the Bank of the United States combined with the then-innovated format for organizing economic power—the corporation. The two seemed to conspire against individual enterprise, manipulating economic outcomes with their mysterious paper transactions and using the federal government to enhance their own fortunes."[38]

In spite of considerable resistance from Congress, in 1832 President Jackson was able to abolish the central bank. It took a willful Treasury Secretary working with Jackson to accomplish the task. Congress had the right to confirm the president's choice of Treasury Secretary, both then and now; and much of Congress was beholden to Wall Street, banking and business interests just as it is today. As a result, Congress tried to keep the central bank alive by refusing to confirm Jackson's choices for Treasury Secretary. Eventually the people won out when Jackson vetoed legislation that would have kept the bank alive.

Between 1833 and 1912, there was no central bank in existence to interfere with American commerce. America was a free country. Then in 1913 a group of powerful bankers that included J.P. Morgan, Paul Warburg and John D. Rockefeller, achieved their fathers' and great grandfathers' goal.[39] [40] Congress passed the Federal Reserve Act establishing another central bank[41]—a private, secretive banking cartel with immense power. Since that fateful year, America has never been the same.[42]

In the early 1990's, U.S. Representative Henry B. Gonzalez (D-TX) chaired the US House of Representatives Financial Services Committee. Gonzalez was ranking member until 1999. Rep. Gonzalez was well aware of the financial carnage that the Federal Reserve and the FDIC had wrought on Texas in the 1980s. Gonzalez conducted an investigation of the Federal Reserve and economist Robert D. Auerbach wrote about the investigation in the book *"Deception and Abuse at the Fed: Henry B. Gonzalez Battles Alan Greenspan's Bank."*[43]

According to Auerbach (and others), the Fed has grown to be an approximately 23,000-person wasteful, bloated bureaucracy with an operating budget exceeding $2 billion, with immense powers to approve or deny the purchase of competitor banks by trillion-dollar banking conglomerates. The Fed controls the nation's money supply and manages targeted interest rates, among other things. The Fed is led by nineteen unelected decision makers: the presidents of each of the twelve Federal Reserve district banks and the seven governors at its Washington, D.C. headquarters that comprise the Board of Governors or the "Board". Twelve of these nineteen officials sit on the Fed's most important policy-making committee, which is the Federal Open Market Committee (FOMC). The seven governors are nominated by the President and must be confirmed by the Senate. Each governor serves a fourteen-year term and they can be fired only through congressional impeachment, which has never happened. One of the seven governors is the Chairman of both central policy-making committees, the FOMC and the Board of Governors. The Chairman is nominated by the President and confirmed by the Senate. He serves a four-year term as chairman and can be reappointed and confirmed for additional terms.[44] [45]

In the 1930s, the Fed allowed the depression to get worse and persist longer than it otherwise would have.[46] The Glass-Steagall Acts were enacted in 1932 and 1933.[47] The 1932 act liberalized the terms for member-bank borrowing from the Fed. The 1933 law, also called the Banking Act, separated commercial banking from underwriting and other activities of investment banks. The Act was intended to restore the public confidence in paper money. The Act established federal deposit insurance and formed the Federal Deposit Insurance Corporation (FDIC).[48] FDIC regulates all banks with federal deposit insurance.[49] In the 1930s, the Feds imposition of strict monetary policy, plus an ill advised foreign policy helped lead to the most catastrophic war in human history.[50]

The 1930s brought Macroeconomics to the nation's economy. With respect to the current national economy, the *Wall Street Journal* recently wrote:[51]

"How did modern economics fly off the rails? The answer is that the 'invisible hand' of the free enterprise system, first explained in 1776 by Adam Smith, got tossed aside for the new 'macroeconomics,' a witchcraft that began to flourish in the 1930s during the rise of Keynes. Macroeconomics simply took basic laws of economics we know to be true for the firm or family—i.e., that demand curves are downward sloping; that when you tax something, you get less of it; that debts have to be repaid—and turned them on their head as national policy.

"As Donald Boudreaux, professor of economics at George Mason University and author of the invaluable blog Cafe Hayek put it: 'Macroeconomics was nothing more than a dismissal of the rules of economics.' Over the years, this has led to some horrific blunders, such as the New Deal decision to pay farmers to burn crops and slaughter livestock to keep food prices high: To encourage food production, destroy it."

In 1944, the Bretton-Woods Agreement established the dollar as the world reserve currency—money used for international transactions—permitting paper notes to be traded for gold bullion at a rate of $35 to one ounce of gold.[52]

It wasn't until 1951 that the Fed was able to tap directly into the U.S. Treasury. During the Korean War, President Truman signed an agreement that allowed the Fed to achieve independence in setting interest rates.[53] The agreement required that the Treasury give up all power to issue money, limiting Treasury's authority to overseeing the Bureau of Engraving and Printing which fulfills the Fed's orders for new currency and coins.[54] The man responsible for this change was Truman's fellow Democrat William McChesney Martin, whom Truman appointed to be Chairman of the Federal Reserve. Later, when Truman realized that he had been tricked, he called Martin a "traitor".[55]

Martin's activities were the catalyst that allowed the Federal Reserve to expand the cartel's sphere of influence in a manner that would engulf and eventually dominate much of the world; by using the American taxpayers' dollars as a private piggy bank that would have to be defended worldwide by the U.S. military, without US citizens and most members of Congress even knowing about it.

There are indications that the infamous Rockefeller interests were able to benefit from Martin's activities while Chairman of the Federal Reserve. In June, 1991, Mr. David Rockefeller, private banker and member of the Council on Foreign Relations was quoted as saying: "We are grateful to the Washington Post, the New York Times, Time Magazine, and other great publications whose directors have attended our meetings and respected their promises of discretion for almost 40 years" ("Almost" forty years before the day of the speech would be about 1952, 1953 or 1954, shortly after Martin's treasonous activities began at the Federal Reserve). Rockefeller continued "It would have been impossible for us to develop our plan for the world if we had been subjected to the lights of publicity during those years. But now the world is more sophisticated and prepared to march towards a world government. The supra national sovereignty of an intellectual elite and world bankers is surely preferable to the national auto-determination practiced in past centuries."[56]

In 1961, during another time of conflict, while President John F. Kennedy was distracted by the Bay of Pigs invasion, William McChesney Martin lent himself to a scheme by the Federal Reserve to circumvent its constitutional authority to appropriate money to foreign interests by engaging in foreign currency and loan activities without congressional approval. According to Robert D. Auerbach:

"In April, 1961, Fed Governor J. L. Robertson (according to paraphrased transcripts) inquired as to the advantages seen— aside from the Federal Reserve's 'unlimited pocketbook'—in having two agencies (the Treasury and the Fed) operating in this field instead of one, and Mr. (Charles A.) Coombs replied that he did not think there were any."[57]

"The need by the government to evade congressional budgetary authority was admitted to be the basic reason for the establishment of the fund for foreign-exchange currency intervention at the Federal Reserve.... Robertson opposed the operation in foreign currencies 'on legal, practical and policy grounds ... because the program was being undertaken without specific congressional approval.'[58]

"Fed Chairman William McChesney Martin, Jr., as Chairman of the Federal Reserve,[59] developed a peculiar, contradictory rationale to justify the absence of a request for formal authorization from Congress: although the Fed had received favorable opinions from its own and the (Kennedy) administration's lawyers, it did not know exactly what it was doing, so it would not know what to ask Congress to authorize. If it truly did not know what it was doing, the pleasing approvals from the lawyers should have been suspect. This disingenuous sophistry was part of a plan to keep Congress uninformed about the Fed's circumvention of its constitutional authority to appropriate money."[60]

Mr. Auerbach then goes on to discuss, in considerable detail in his book, the extensive efforts that the Federal Reserve went to in order to transfer the taxpayer's money to its own accounts while continuing to deceive Congress.

For two centuries, American's economic growth and military strength had been based on adherence to Constitutional law; sound trade policies; "American values"; loyalties; strong work ethic; good educational system; small business; ingenuity; business and finance mechanisms; fair labor policies; and the individual freedoms and initiatives of the nation's people including inventors, manufacturers and engineers. Then came the 1960s and the change was implemented with the assassination of President John F. Kennedy.

In 1964, Fed Chairman Martin threatened to end the practice of preparing transcripts of FOMC meetings. The transcripts were called "Memorandum of Discussions" (MODs). The transcripts had been prepared for internal use since 1936.[61] This act appears to be the beginning of the now decades-long Fed policy of concealing records of its activities, including its activities involving insider trading.

The power given to Congress to appropriate federal governmental funds is specified in the Constitution: "No money shall be drawn from the Treasury but in consequence of appropriations made by law" (article I, section 9). Nevertheless, beginning 1962, the FOMC had voted to lend money to foreign countries through "swap lines"[62] [63] or "swap drawings", and in recent decades, voted to "warehouse" funds for the U.S. Treasury so that the Treasury could avoid limits on the funds available to it from congressional authorization.[64] By utilizing its foreign-exchange business, the Fed has facilitated an insider trading apparatus involving fifty-eight foreign and domestic institutions, out of sight of Congress and the American taxpayer.

For example, according to Auerbach, "During a five-year period beginning about 1989 the Fed had transacted foreign-exchange business with fifty-eight foreign and domestic institutions including private banks and brokerages. The Fed would call these parties and tell them to buy billions of dollars of a currency, say U.S. dollars. The foreign entities received very valuable information that they could exploit for enormous profits."[65]

Auerbach also wrote: "Information about plans by the Federal Reserve to change interest rates could be turned into huge profits if it were known before the policy was made public. And it is wishful thinking to pretend that millions, easily billions, of dollars have not been made using just such inside information from the Fed. The Fed's secrets have been widely disseminated to its employees and the favored few. People who have never had the limited background check that a new Fed employee receives, including members of foreign central banks from Russia and China as well as academics from the United States, have been admitted to these secret meetings.

"With such information, a person could buy a security in a market outside the United States, such as a bond futures contract, and the asset could be sold for a higher price after the Fed moves and bond prices rise. These securities may be purchased for less than half a percent of their face value in cash, generating a very large profit in one day from a drop in interest rates. Rather than directly take a position in the market, a leaker or the favored leakee could sell the information to others. Similar activities at private sector corporations would be treated as crimes."[66]

Fed secrecy continues to the present day. In the 1990s, President Clinton's efforts to open up the Fed were apparently disappointing to Fed officials. A few Democrats and Republicans began to close ranks against the Fed; however, Clinton Attorney General Janet Reno steered the investigation to an ineffective Fed inspector general and Fed appeasement continued. This is the evasive tactic that Americans could most likely expect from a new President Perry, a new President Romney, a new President Cain or a new President Gingrich.

Congressman Ron Paul was out of Congress at the time of the Gonzalez investigation. When Paul tried to become reelected to his old House seat in 1996, the Republican National Committee and both House Speaker Newt Gingrich and then-Texas Governor George W. Bush urged a Texas Democrat to change parties and run against Paul in his home district during the Republican primary, apparently doing whatever they could do to protect the Federal Reserve from audit once Congressman Gonzalez had retired. Ron Paul won anyway. Then the AFL-CIO, whose leadership is rumored to also receive money or insider trading information from the Fed, gave vast sums of money to Texas Democrat Charles "Lefty" Morris in the general election, and Paul beat him too.

Now U.S. Representative Ron Paul holds the same banking chairmanship in the U.S. House as Gonzalez once did, and Paul is also running for president with full intention of ordering an audit of the Federal Reserve. Paul also appears to know what Rick Perry, Mitt Romney, Herman Cain, Newt Gingrich and Chris Christi are all up to and their reasons for campaigning for election to high office in 2012. It has become obvious that those candidates are there to try to dilute Ron Paul's support, because those candidates are directly or indirectly supported by the Fed and they will protect the Fed from audit if elected.

The Fed continues to engage in foreign operations without Congressional authorization. Those foreign operations, including those of the American commercial banks, continue to have an adverse impact on the American banking system and economy, dragging the nation into what could become another Great Depression.

7

PAUL VOLCKER, THE GEORGE BUSHES,
AND THE MEXICAN MAFIA

If ye love wealth better than liberty, the tranquility of servitude
better than the animating contest of freedom, go home from us
in peace. We ask not your counsels or arms. Crouch down
and lick the hands which feed you. May your chains sit lightly
upon you, and may posterity forget that ye were our
countrymen!

~ Samuel Adams

The current financial crisis did not begin with President Obama or even former President George W. Bush. Nor did it begin with former Presidents Clinton, H.W. Bush, or Reagan. It began slowly during the Carter presidency, when President Carter appointed Paul Volcker to head the Federal Reserve. It was Volcker and an activist Congress that together were willing to sacrifice the manufacturing strength of the country—the basis of the economy that had made the nation so powerful in the world.

On August 15, 1971, Richard Nixon's presidential pen had fallen under the watchful eye of economist Paul Volcker. Taking Volcker's advice,[67] Nixon signed the nation away from its basis for money—the gold standard. According to William Greider:

"Under Nixon, Volcker worked closely with Treasury Secretary John Connally, an urbane Texas politician who frequently complained about Volcker's dowdy appearance.

Together Connally and Volcker engineered the most fundamental change in the world's monetary system since World War II—the dismantling of the Bretton Woods agreement that had made the US dollar the stable benchmark for all currencies. The changes that began in 1971 meant the final abandonment of gold as a US guarantee behind its money and the introduction of floating exchange rates among the world's major currencies. Some critics still condemned Volcker bitterly for his role in those reforms, but he himself had originally argued for preserving the system of fixed exchange rates."[68]

By the 1970s, domestic social engineering programs enacted by the U.S. Congress, and the Federal Reserve gambling large amounts of taxpayer dollars in the international markets, resulted in a substantial national debt with little chance of repayment. The Federal Reserve then started increasing the rate of inflation by printing money on a massive scale—but nowhere as massive as the scale of money being printed now under the Obama administration.

Volcker's Federal Reserve, along with the U.S. Congress, and the giant banks of New York along with Wall Street, accelerated the financing of the globalist agenda of international elitists controlling international economies—controlling the means of method of production of the entire world—the madman scenario dreamed about by dictatorial tyrants since the world began.

By the late 1970s, business and manufacturing corporations entered their worst economic slump in a quarter century as lower cost foreign producers drained away export markets. The Texas petrochemical industry had boomed for decades by producing building plastics, but during the 1970s more cost-efficient overseas competitors began eating away at its export markets for bulk petrochemicals. The operating rate of the U.S. petrochemical industry, about half of which is located on Texas Gulf Coast, plunged to 50 percent of capacity.[69]

Paul Volcker took the oath of office to be chairman of the Federal Reserve on August 6, 1979. On March 31, 1980 President Carter signed the newly-enacted Depository Institution Deregulation and

Monetary Control Act PL 96-221, leading the nation's economy down the dark path that exists today.

The bill was shepherded through Congress by Representative Fernand J. St. Germain, Senator Jake Garn and Paul Volcker. The Act gave new powers to the Federal Reserve System, thereby converting America's business system from manufacturing into the creation of credit or debt. The Act also lowered (banking) reserve requirements from one hundred percent to three percent and overrode state usury laws and interest rate limitations.[70]

Mr. William Greider makes specific reference to state usury laws in his book. Usury can be defined as "profit obtained through interest-bearing loans that involve exploitation of the economically weak by the strong and resourceful. It is an exploitation characterized by the fact that the lender, while retaining full ownership of the capital loaned and having no legal concern with the purpose for which it is to be used or with the manner of its use, remains contractually assured of gain, regardless of any losses that the borrower may suffer in consequence of the transaction."

Up until 1980, state usury laws had protected economically weak Americans. With the new federal law overriding all state usury laws, financial usury hit the nation's citizens with a vengeance. History tells us that Communist leaders Marx and Engels had written the Communist Manifesto based on the power and influence exerted through usury that had become the catalyst of the French Revolution.

The Act also increased risk to the U.S. taxpayer, which resulted in what is now known in banking circles as a system of large banks and businesses that are "too big to fail." According to Greider: "The Act also increased FDIC deposit insurance coverage by 150 percent from $40,000 to $100,000, thereby allowing banks and savings and loans to draw in vast sums of taxpayer insured cash,[71] which was a provision added by St. Germain in the late hours without debate."[72]

The Federal Reserve, with the assistance of the U.S. Congress, EPA and a burdensome income tax system, had pushed America's manufacturing and engineering into a "globalist" world trade system, while increasing the pressure on the world's economies to repay the Federal Reserve, New York banks, Wall Street investors and politicians of   various stripes. Now all over the planet, central banks buy off the politicians and seize the water, the roads, the power plants and other infrastructure.[73]

The American mega-banks had gambled and loaned money to foreign nations all over the world, greedily drawing in billions of dollars of interest payments. But, by the early 1980s, the foreign nations could not repay. Rather than allow the foreign governments to default on the debt, the nation's financiers chose to make the American taxpayer pay the debt instead. Many foreign nations would need to be propped up by the embattled American taxpayer in order to enable the New York banks to survive. Simultaneously, trillions of dollars in private American assets would need to be seized from individuals by the government in such a manner that few people would recognize what was happening to them.

The United States became the world's policemen, with a military presence in over 130 countries throughout the world, as the United States Federal Reserve exerted financial controls on other nations. From the *Wall Street Journal*:

"With the loans came the U.S. government's political mandates on foreign governments. For example, El Salvador outsourced monetary policy to the Fed, and Salvadorans left themselves vulnerable to (the Fed chairman's) weakness as a central banker. The effects of dollar inflation are felt here more intensely than in the U.S. El Salvador once had its own vibrant agricultural sector, but agrarian reform imposed by the U.S. ... destroyed the large, efficient farm and left rural communities destitute. So at a time when U.S. agriculture was consolidating and mechanizing, a model of primitive, postage-stamp farming—less than 500 hectares per farm— was forced on El Salvador. Agriculture has never fully recovered.... Washington is now pushing a new 'equality' agenda to require El Salvador to complicate the tax code to force Salvadorians to pay more taxes. As a result, tax and regulatory burden for entrepreneurs is stifling, particularly for small and medium sized businesses."[74]

The success of capitalism for the few controllers of wealth in the United States depends on an abundant supply of cheap labor (and the flow of illegal immigrants across the nation's borders). Volcker wanted wages to fall. "In crude terms, Volcker and the Federal Reserve were determined to 'break labor'," according to Greider.[75] "The Federal Reserve became like a State Department for finance, independently capable of arranging huge international credit transactions and prevailing on other central banks to go along. The Federal Reserve under Volcker, as journalist Joseph Kraft put it, formed a kind of 'Mexican mafia' within the US government."[76]

By 1980, with Mexico's economy already undermined by Federal Reserve meddling, the primary focus of the New York invaders turned to seizure of America's west-Texas oil and gas assets. The First National Bank of Midland, Texas was their primary target. Midland is located within the heart of the Permian Basin, a rich oil and gas field that contains some of the largest known reserves in the United States. The bank was the largest independent energy bank in Texas.

In the early 1980s, the United States imported very little oil and even less natural gas. The Saudis controlled OPEC and, almost as if planned (and many in Texas believe it was indeed planned), in late 1982 OPEC collapsed the price of oil being shipped to the United States, thereby collapsing the price of oil sold by U.S. producers. When America's small and mid-sized independent oil producers turned to Congress for help, Congress refused to provide any assistance or "price floor"[77] for the domestic energy industry. The independent oil and gas industry began to rapidly fail. The national unemployment rate reached 10.5 percent in the final quarter of 1982. Farm foreclosures began and working-man wages declined. For the most part, the large multinational oil companies stayed offshore, out of the way of the financial carnage taking place in America's domestic energy business.

The Federal Reserve decided it would use the smaller, solvent American banks to help rescue both Mexico as well as rescue the largest American banks. Mexico, with all the money it owed to the New York banks, was considered to be of higher priority than the energy security of the United States.

Greider noted: "Between Friday, August 13, 1982 and Monday,

August 16, 1982, the Federal Reserve and the U.S. Department of Energy agreed to bail out Mexico's debt to the New York banks. The DOE agreed to buy $1 billion of oil from Mexico and to pay in advance immediately, instead of paying on delivery. In addition, the Dept of Agriculture provided another $1 billion line of credit for the future purchase of U.S. grain and other food products. Volcker organized a $1.85 billion loan pool among the central banks of the industrial world, half of the money to be provided by the Fed. Mexico, in effect, was now in receivership to the international financiers. When the world's markets opened on Monday morning, there was no crisis, no reason to panic. Very few figures in American politics questioned the intervention. Many drew a deep breath and applauded."[78]

"(Six months later), a dozen or more debtor nations were lining up seeking the equivalent of Chapter 11 bankruptcy protection, and one by one the IMF negotiated 'work out' plans for the failed debtors, forcing the sovereign nations to accept the banker's terms. The process of debt rescheduling for the less developed nations was not essentially different from the refinancing plans that commercial banks had worked out for such major corporate debtors as International Harvester when it approached failure the year before. Only the stakes were many times larger, especially for the banks. Just as Harvester was too big to fail, too deeply in debt, so were the leading borrowers of Latin America. Letting them fail would bring down the largest banks in the country, but rescheduling of old debts did not solve the fundamental problems facing Latin American debtors."[79]

In order to finance the bailouts, the Federal Reserve and Volcker pressured the midsize and smaller American banks to loan their money to foreign countries. By the spring of 1983, President Ronald Reagan smelled what Volcker and his Federal Reserve cronies were up to. According to Greider, "Donald Regan confided that he and President Reagan had actually discussed abolishing the Fed. Jim Baker was also very reluctant to reappoint Volcker."[80]

Reagan threatened to fire Volcker when Volcker's term was up. Meetings were held between officials of the Federal Reserve and the First National Bank of Midland's directors in Washington, DC. Vice President George H.W. Bush had decades of contacts within the directorship of the First National Bank. Several of the bank's directors were listed in Forbes and were among the wealthiest Americans.

The vice-president's son, George W. Bush, was in Midland trying to learn the energy exploration and development business. It was during this period that the young Bush became a useful tool for protecting one of the largest depositors at First National—Merrill Lynch—the same Merrill Lynch that the Federal Reserve forced Bank of America to buy in 2008 at the beginning of the present economic crisis that finalized the younger Bush presidency.

George W. Bush's association with a failing bank was too much for President Reagan. The indication is that Reagan was threatened by the Fed's intention to use a hostile Media against him, and Reagan would be a one-term president. The fix went in. Volcker kept his job and President Reagan was later reelected for a second term. The First National Bank of Midland collapsed in October 1983 and at the time it was the second largest failure in U.S. banking history. In 1982, the Federal Reserve and OCC had provided ample warning to select stockholders so that they could sell their stock as quietly as possible. The quiet looting of the bank was underway. Later, after the bank had failed, the FDIC refused to collect amounts owed by the wealthy former bank directors. Alliances and deals had been made. The stench of bribes and blackmail whiffed through the west Texas air all the way to New York and Washington, DC.

Texas was not the only state devastated by the Federal Reserve's fraudulent policies in the 1980s. Oklahoma, Louisiana, New Mexico, Colorado and California were hit hard as well. Throughout the nation's heartland the Federal Reserve destroyed the family farm and FDIC then sold the land to large agribusiness corporations allowing the farmers to work as tenant farmers on the land that they had used to own. Mr. William Greider wrote:

"For every borrower who had overreached and was subsequently crushed by debt, there was a willing banker who also had been too optimistic, who had made the same bet. It was simply not rational to condemn one side of the debt transaction as reckless and sympathize with the other

61

side as an unfortunate victim. Yet the government rushed to assist the lenders who had been burned and, simultaneously, left the borrowers to their fate. This moral confusion between debtors and lenders was especially evident at the Federal Reserve. The central bank successfully evaded any real public responsibility for what was happening to American farmers and other debtors, much as it had turned aside the complaints from Midwestern farmers destroyed in the Fed's deflation back in the 1920s. The exhaustive press and television coverage on the plight of the failing farmers almost never mentioned any connection with monetary policy or the Federal Reserve.[81]

"Catastrophe was general in Iowa. Thousands of farmers faced liquidation on old debts or their banks refused to grant new credit for the approaching growing season. The value of Iowa farmland was decreased by half and small towns withered as the local commerce disappeared. The Middle West and other regions were trapped in an economic phenomenon beyond the living experience of most Americans—deflation. Farmers decided their plight was caused by a remote conspiracy of bankers, operating through the Federal Reserve. "First the Powers pump up inflation, then they start the propaganda that we have to reduce inflation" said one. "They established this policy for the personal gain of the Federal Reserve and the bankers that control it. They saw the coffee shortage, the oil shortage, the sugar shortage. The Powers found out that it works. Why not a money shortage...? Even in the Bible, you're not supposed to have usury. It's usury that's killing us."[82]

Congress also changed income tax accounting rules. Instead of the new changes taking place over a period of time, they took place all at once. Thousands of apartment properties around the nation no longer made economic sense to their owners, so the owners either walked away or filed bankruptcy. Banks with apartment property loans then failed. The FDIC foreclosed and sold off the assets to Wall Street "vulture" companies that either held them or sold them to others at significant profits.

Texans learned their lesson in the 1980s: don't trust the Federal Reserve, don't trust the New York banks, and don't trust the federal government, especially when the government says "we are here to help you," which actually to employers means that "we are here to control you or destroy you." That knowledge is how many employers in Texas have kept their businesses open during the current financial crisis, and some have been creating new jobs; but many employers are still very wary, especially those working in the oil industry.

By the late 1980s, the Federal Reserve's policies had effectively moved millions of manufacturing jobs overseas, crashing the stock market in the process as one man's loss became another man's gain. The dollar's international value had been driven higher by the increases in interest rates in the early 1980s, and by the end of the decade the nation's competitive worldwide-advantage in the international market had been eliminated. America had become a borrower nation, thanks to Congress and the Federal Reserve.

Severely impacted were all the trade-sensitive sectors of the American economy—from farming to autos to machine tools. Mr. Greider wrote: "Lee Iacocca of Chrysler summarized the overall losses from the strong dollar. Addressing a Washington audience, Iacocca warned: 'People in this town better start realizing that buried somewhere in those numbers, between the highs and lows of these dollar swings, are things like 140,000 bankruptcies, three million jobs going overseas and 100,000 fewer farmers, most of whom lost their land. These aren't just bell curves from a textbook. These are real people, human beings trying to eat and buy shoes for their kids and pay off the mortgage.' "[83]

Greider also wrote: "Americans asked who was to blame for the unfortunate devastation—the Federal Reserve or the executive branch and Congress. The Federal Reserve succeeded in evading the blame as finger pointing went in all directions. The ambiguity posed the sort of fine-grain question that policy analysts in Washington enjoyed studying. Their conclusions were invariably carefully hedged assessments of cause and effect. For the millions of citizens and business enterprises that suffered the consequences, a simpler answer was sufficient: the U.S. government was to blame, all of it."[84]

It was most likely known in the hallways of the Federal Reserve that something had to be done to conceal the Fed's globalist ambitions. It would take another twenty years to bring about the New World Order to full fruition. In the early 1990s, the American people would be deceived by a new housing boom that would include the added feature of creative financing and buying a house with no money down. It did not matter if the borrower could pay the money back. There was big money to be made in housing construction loans and mortgages that could be packaged and sold upstream to the suckers on Wall Street and in Europe while China bought the nation's debt.

It would not be until November, 2008, near the end of the presidency of George W. Bush, that the financial charade would manifest itself with another stock market crash and loss of millions of jobs.

8

❦ FEAR AND LOATHING IN THE MEDIA ❧

With a fascist the problem is never how best to present the truth to the public but how best to use the news to deceive the public into giving the fascist and his group more money or more power.

~ Henry A. Wallace

The global elite have consolidated massive power over the last several decades. Global corporations not only fund and develop large multi-technical projects both in the United States and abroad, they also own the major news media. As a result, Americans are manipulated daily on a mass scale as to what to believe and desire, both socially and politically.

Edward Bernays, the nephew of world famous psychoanalyst Sigmund Freud, studied group dynamics and became the "father of public relations." In 1928, Bernays authored the book *Propaganda* in which he described how to intelligently and constantly manipulate the habits and opinions of the masses within a democratic society. Bernays went on to state that "Those who harness this unseen mechanism of society, constitute an invisible government and are the true ruling power. It is they who control the wires that control the public mind and harness old social forces and find new ways to bind and guide the world."[85]

The owners and directors of America's major news media have reason to fear the Federal Reserve. The Fed operates in secrecy and has the power to make or break a bank without disclosing its true intentions for doing so. The Fed also has the power to make or break a business of any size, including any major news organization, through the Fed's control of the banks.

The New York banks, with the cooperation of the Federal Reserve and large international banks and investment funds, help major news media enterprises consolidate their power through media acquisition of smaller rivals and competitors. The end result is that the news media that once functioned as the American people's watchdog protector against government abuse and tyranny is no more.

Aaron Russo was a filmmaker and rock-musician promoter who successfully promoted musicians, such as Janis Joplin; and bands, such as Jefferson Airplane, The Grateful Dead and The Who. Russo produced films including *Trading Places*, *The Rose* and a masterpiece documentary titled: *America: Freedom to Fascism*.[86]

Russo also became friends with Nicholas Rockefeller of the infamous Rockefeller banking and business dynasty, maintaining a close personal friendship with Rockefeller but eventually ending the relationship appalled by what he had learned about the Rockefellers and their ambitions. Russo described his relationship with Nicholas Rockefeller in this manner:[87]

"I got a call one day from an attorney woman I knew, and she said 'Would you like to meet one of the Rockefellers?' And I said 'Sure, I'd love to.' And we became friends. And he began to divulge a lot of things to me. So he said to me one night (eleven months before September 11, 2001), he said that 'There's going to be an event Aaron. And out of that event, you're going to see we are going to go into Afghanistan so we can run pipelines from the Caspian Sea. We're going to go into Iraq to take the oil and establish a base in the Middle East. And we're going to go into Venezuela and try to get rid of Chavez.' And the first two they've accomplished, Chavez they didn't accomplish.

"And you see guys going into caves looking for people that they're never going to find. He's laughing about the fact that you have this war on terror. There's no real enemy. He's talking about how by having this war on terror, you can never win it because it is this eternal war. And so you can always keep taking people's liberties away. And I said 'How are you going to convince people that this war is real?' And he said 'The Media—the Media can convince everybody that this is real. You keep talking about things. You keep saying it over and over and over again. And eventually people believe it.'

"You know you created the Federal Reserve in 1913 through lies. You create 9/11 which is another lie. Thru 9/11 ... then you're fighting a war on terror. Now all of a sudden you go into Iraq which is another lie. And now they're going to do Iran. You know. And so one thing leading to another, leading to another, leading to another.

"And I say 'What are you doing this for? Why are you doing this thing? What's the point of this thing? You have all the money you could want. You want all the power,' and I said 'You know you're hurting people. It's not a good thing.' And he'd say 'What do you care about the people for. Take care of yourself and take care of your family.' And I said to him 'What are the ultimate goals here?' He said 'the ultimate goal is to give everyone in this world an RFID chip, and to have all money be on those chips and everything on those chips. And if anyone wants to protest what we do or violate what we want, we just turn off their chip."

The Federal Reserve also controls routine operations of the news media with regard to any reporting about the Fed. For example, as Mr. Auerbach explains in his book, former Fed Chairman Alan Greenspan did not hold formal press conferences. He held off-the-record conferences only with selected reporters. As Laurence Meyer explains, "The use of reporters as part of the Fed's signal corps is not official Board or FOMC doctrine." Meyer describes the practice and notes that the public-affairs staff and Greenspan "like to pretend it doesn't happen." He typically relies on a small group of reporters. John Berry, longtime reporter for *The Washington Post* and at *Bloomberg,* is most widely recognized in this role. "The Wall Street Journal reporter covering the Fed—it was David Wessel, then Jake Schlesinger, and most recently Greg Ip during my term—was also a regular member of the signal corps."[88]

Auerbach notes that individual reporters are likely to consider their inclusion in this kind of selective access important for their employment, although exclusion awaits the reporters if their reports include criticism of the Fed. After Jim McTague, Washington editor of *Barron's,* wrote a column that suggested that Fed policy had contributed to the defeat of President George H.W. Bush, he was told that he was banned from further conferences with Greenspan.[89]

Freedom of the Press seemed to almost completely disappear in the 1980s as the major news media corporations expanded their size and powers. Americans turned away from the three traditional major network corporations and expanded their horizons to news by way of satellite and Internet.

The financial world decides which political candidates or existing office holders are to receive favorable news media treatment and which ones do not. The news media enterprises are paid handsomely each election cycle in the form of huge advertising dollars to perpetuate and control the American political thought and selection process, and also to help control the people who are elected to serve. If a political candidate or elected official is already known nationwide as someone who wants the Fed to be audited, that person is regarded as a threat to the Fed, and the media does everything it can do to either discredit or ignore the existence of that person.

William Greider, whose background was in the news media, offered some comments on the major news media and its relationship to the Federal Reserve with regard to President Reagan:

"The major news media always defers to the interests of the Federal Reserve. About April 6, 1984, the Federal Reserve Board raised its Discount rate to 9 percent, the first change since December 1982. The Reagan White House protested, yet Volcker brushed the White House comments aside as political complaints. The bankers congratulated the Federal Reserve governors on their recent tightening, taking note of 'the highly charged political atmosphere' and warned that this turbulence 'increases the contribution that monetary policy must make to maintaining confidence.... Politicians were expected to defer to the higher judgment of economics —a standard enforced by the news media which criticized the White House for meddling in the Fed's decisions."[90]

"Had the news media been interested in doing a proper job of reporting the news, the Federal Reserve's decision to halt the recovering economy might have provoked great controversy, especially since the decision was made by an obscure group of unelected Federal Reserve technocrats in defiance of the President's wishes and in the midst of an election campaign. Yet there was no public outcry. Of all the institutions of Washington, none was more deferential toward the Federal Reserve than the press, and the press was not about to report the significance of what the Fed was doing to the economy, not then and not even later when the effects of the Fed's tightening were fully visible."[91]

"The major news media fights reform of the Federal Reserve. The Republican Party, in 1984, adopted in its platform a section inspired by Representative Jack Kemp, which called for reform of the Federal Reserve and a return to the gold standard. The press ignored this one too. Money seemed too complicated to understand or to explain."[92]

Fox News chief Roger Ailes helped Rupert Murdoch launch Fox News in 1996. Ailes worked as a strategist for Republican Presidents Richard Nixon, Ronald Reagan and George H. W. Bush.[93] According to a report from Yahoo!'s John Cook, News Corp. minority shareholder Saudi Prince Al-Waleed bin Talal directly funded (Imam Feisal Abdul) Rauf's project to build a Muslim community center and mosque near Ground Zero in Manhattan. News Corp. is the parent company of Fox News.[94]

Fox News exerted its influence to protect Governor Rick Perry at an early date. In Texas, the 2010 Republican three-candidate primary race for governor evolved into a "winner take all" race that featured Governor Rick Perry, U.S. Senator Kay Bailey Hutchison, and Debra Medina—a Tea Party candidate. Medina had become involved in politics in the 1990s; had become Wharton County, Texas GOP charwoman in 2004; and had served as Interim State Coordinator for the *Campaign for Liberty*. In 2008, she decided to run for governor.[95]

Medina was also a high-level volunteer for U.S. Representative Ron Paul's 2008 presidential campaign, and Paul is very popular in Texas. Candidate Governor Rick Perry was in trouble with his poll numbers, as was Senator Hutchison, who had conducted a very weak campaign. Medina's popularity rose rapidly in the polls and there were rumors that Hutchison had entered the race to be a "spoiler" to split the Republican vote and to keep Medina from defeating Rick Perry.

On February 11, 2010, Fox News commentator Glenn Beck undertook a media ambush of Medina. During a radio interview, Beck told Medina that he had received emails saying that she was a "9/11 truther" without Medina even being able to see the emails. Medina failed to specifically deny the charge. She indicated that she didn't have an opinion on the matter, saying that some good questions had been raised about the issue, and said that the American people had not seen all the evidence. According to writer Jacob B. Hornberger, "After the interview was over, Beck and his on-air cohorts began yucking it up, scratching off any prospects for Medina, who had recently soared from 4 percent in the polls to 24 percent, to possibly eventually win the Texas race. 'Wow' Beck exclaimed. 'The fastest way back to four percent. I think I can write her off the list'."[96]

Beck had apparently not really been interested in Medina's position on 9/11 controversies. Instead, Beck was employing one of Saul Alinski's socialistic/Marxist Rules for Radicals which is "Whenever possible, go outside the experience of an opponent. Here you want to cause confusion, fear, and retreat."[97] Medina explained her position to supporters after the show, but the damage had already been done. Rick

Perry was eventually elected to another term as governor.

In April 2010, Beck and Governor Rick Perry scheduled an on-stage town hall-style event together in Tyler, Texas. An article noted that Beck had played a "special role" in the Republican gubernatorial primary. According to the article, "He (Beck) had candidate Debra Medina on his radio show and asked her if she was a '9/11 truther.' When he didn't like Medina's answer, Beck said, 'Rick, I think you and I could French kiss right now.' Medina's campaign never recovered."[98]

On April 16, 2010, an article noted that Ron Paul supporters were abandoning Beck in droves, and Becks 2010 ratings at Fox News had hit a new low.[99] On August 19, 2010, Michael Wolff reported that Rupert Murdock or Roger Ailes had donated a million dollars to the Republican Governors Association,[100] of which Governor Rick Perry has served as chairman.

In 2009, Fox News and Glenn Beck had heavily promoted the "Tea Party" grass roots campaign, but by 2011 Fox News was trying to distance itself from the movement.[101] Meanwhile, Beck continued to try to inspire viewers with discussions of America's founding fathers, American history and the Constitution, and eventually the topic of the rise of the Federal Reserve. In April 2011, Beck devoted his entire show to a discussion of the Federal Reserve with guest author G. Edward Griffin, who had written *The Creature from Jekyll Island*, a critique of modern economic theory and practice, specifically a criticism of the Federal Reserve System.[102]

The producers at Fox News then apparently decided that they had had enough. Mention of the Federal Reserve was near verboten among the major news media, but here was a well-known author who for many years had criticized the Fed and written a famous book—and here he was on Beck's show! Roger Ailes and Glenn Beck then parted ways.[103]

More recently, Fox News has engaged in a large number of dirty tricks against presidential candidate Ron Paul.[104] The Federal Reserve continues to deceive Congress and the American taxpayers, and also appears to be extremely worried about U.S. Representative Ron Paul's efforts to have the Federal Reserve audited. The mainstream media, obviously acting like they are under the control of the New York banking industry and the Federal Reserve, are doing whatever they can to avoid mentioning Ron Paul's presidential candidacy at all, much less mention Representative Paul's name in a positive light.

Ron Paul achieved a historic finish at the Iowa Straw Poll, coming in a close second to Tea Party candidate Michele Bachmann. However, the news media clamped a near total blackout on Paul's showing in the race.

None of the media wants anyone to become President of the United States who might break apart the decades-long financial gravy train that the Federal Reserve has lavished on the media corporations and politicians. Persons expressing anti-Federal Reserve points of view are usually derided in the mainstream corporate press as "conspiracy theorists."[105] But that's another Saul Alinski tactic. President George W. Bush derided people who opposed a NAFTA Superhighway through Texas as also being "conspiracy theorists."

Nevertheless, many members of the House of Representatives and a few members of the U.S. Senate are now climbing onto Representative Ron Paul's bandwagon to audit the Fed—at least that's what they are saying before election-day.

9

❧ CASH, CORRUPTION, AND CORPORATISM ❧

The first truth is that the liberty of a democracy is not safe if the people tolerate the growth of private power to a point where it becomes stronger than their democratic state itself. That, in its essence, is fascism—ownership of government by an individual, by a group, or by any other controlling private power.... Among us today a concentration of private power without equal in history is growing.

~ Franklin D. Roosevelt

Governor Rick Perry's political record in Texas shows that he expected the representatives of some of the largest business groups and corporations in Texas to finance his campaigns. Now with Perry on the national stage running for president, if past experience is any guide, Perry most likely expects his campaign to be financed by the largest business groups and corporations in the world.

According to *The Rick Perry Primer* by Texans for Public Justice (TPJ),[106] as of July 2011, Rick Perry had raised $102 million for his Texans for Rick Perry state campaign committee from 2001 through 2010. Half of the money came from 204 individuals and PACs that contributed $100,000 or more including $4,000,000 from the Republican Governors Association PAC; $2,531,799 from Houston homebuilder Bob Perry (no relation to Rick Perry) and wife, and $1,120,000 from Harold C. Simmons of Contran Corporation.

Most American elected officials can usually find themselves under scrutiny when suspected of violation of public trust. Many American

73

businesses adopt standards of conduct restricting the actions of their employees who deal with public officials. The standards are intended to help the business avoid the appearance of impropriety. Some corporations adopt a global anti-bribery and anti-corruption policy. The standards of conduct and policy generally prohibit employees from offering, giving, soliciting or accepting bribes or kickbacks, either in cash or in the form of any other thing or service of value.

Nevertheless, there is always the public official who will take a bribe in the form of a campaign contribution. CREW is an organization that publishes a list of the reputed most corrupt members of Congress. According to CREW, "It's clear that the system for holding accountable those members of Congress who sacrifice the public interest for special interests is not working. Whether members take bribes, violate gift rules, or flout campaign finance regulations, those charged with enforcement often look the other way."[107]

CREW lists as examples politicians such as former Illinois Governor Rod Blagojevich and his alleged attempt to sell Obama's former senate seat; Senator Roland Burris (D-IL) and his three separate explanations for his appointment to the same seat; Representative Jesse Jackson, Jr. (D-IL) who allegedly offered to raise lots of money for the governor if he was appointed to the seat; Representative Ken Calvert (R-CA) who allegedly supported legislation that would benefit him financially; Representative Nathan Deal (R-GA) who allegedly took advantage of a no-bid contract; Representative Jerry Lewis (R-CA) who allegedly steered millions of dollars in government appropriations to his family and friends in exchange for campaign contributions; and Senator Mitch McConnell (R-KY) who allegedly steered earmarks to Gordon Hunter Bates, who was once the senator's chief of staff and a Kentucky lobbyist. According to CREW, Bates clients ("Bates Capitol") include several companies that have received earmarks thanks to the senator, and that have allegedly "made substantial contributions to Sen. McConnell's campaigns."

During earlier times, elected officials would be reelected based on the amount of patronage they could send back to their districts. In two *New York Times* columns, Nobel Prize-winning economist Paul Krugman claimed that Franklin Roosevelt's New Deal was free from corruption, and that it was likely that President Obama, too, could have an honest administration that will take good care of the taxpayer's money as if it were their own. In an article *Welfare Corruption in the New Deal*,[108] author Jim Powell disputed that assertion. Powell wrote: "Truth be told, the New Deal did have some issues. Congress passed the Federal Emergency Relief Act (FERA) on May 12, 1933. Roosevelt's friend Harry Hopkins was sworn in as the chief administrator of the program. FERA had some 150,000 administrative jobs, and there was a mad scramble to control the patronage. As a result, FERA involved government bureaucracies loaded with political hacks and crooks."

According to Powell, "Gov. William Langer of North Dakota was convicted of misappropriating FERA funds and went to prison. Lorena Hickok, Hopkin's chief field representative, reported, 'Texas is a god-awful mess. As you know, they're having a big political fight in Austin ... there's been nothing but delay, confusion, and politics— politics first, last, and always'."

The scramble among politicians from Pennsylvania to New Mexico, from Indiana to New York, from Kentucky to the western states was everywhere, as the rush for taxpayer dollars from the WPA became an important factor in building Democratic organizations in the cities through work relief patronage. As the Democratic machine grew in power in Pittsburgh, the anti-New Deal mayor futilely protested, "Who is going against Santa Claus?" wrote Powell. "In New York there were many reported cases where relief and public-works money were directed not to the neediest but to political supporters." Buying influence was the politics of the day.

Powell noted that Texas Congressman Lyndon B. Johnson, a big admirer of Roosevelt, "advanced his political career by finding jobs for his supporters as well as the supporters of fellow congressmen. Johnson did not gain political influence by turning down incompetent job seekers who wanted government work. Nor did he concede that taxpayers' money might be better spent in another congressman's district. Nor did he believe money would be spent most effectively if taxpayers could keep it and make spending decisions themselves. Power was the name of the Washington game, then as now."

Some politicians seek money from employees, and if the employee does not pay, then he or she might be out of a job. CREW noted one politician, Rep. Vern Buchannan (R-FL) who owned several car dealerships in Florida and who allegedly pressured his employees to make donations to his campaign, in some cases reimbursing them. "In one seven-day period, he raised $110,000 from employees of his numerous car dealerships," CREW reported.

In a manner similar to that of former Governor Ron Blagojevich, Governor Rick Perry has been more than willing to exert pressure on businesspeople in order to receive campaign cash in exchange for his appointments to boards and commissions; however, Blagojevich's expected compensation for favors would be considered "small potatoes" when compared to the campaign contributions that Rick Perry receives.

What do large contributors expect from Governor Rick Perry? Special favors and business advantage from Perry's choices of people to sit on the state's boards and commissions.

Governor Perry has been accused of being a "corporatist" in Texas. According to U.S. Representative Ron Paul, "Corporatism is a system where businesses are nominally in private hands, but are in fact controlled by the government. In a corporatist state, government officials often act in collusion with their favored business interests to design policies that give those interests a monopoly position, to the detriment of both competitors and consumers."[109]

For example, Texas state government controls environmental enforcement through the Texas Commission of Environmental Quality (TCEQ). The governor appoints the TCEQ board. Assume that a businessperson applies to the TCEQ for a construction permit, and some members of the board are opposed to the permit. Whether or not the board is acting rationally, or simply doesn't like the applicant, the Commission turns the businessperson down and he fails to get his permit. In Governor Rick Perry's kingdom, if the businessperson wants to establish a business that requires state approval, even a monopoly on a particular business enterprise, the businessperson is expected to contribute money to the governor's campaigns. The governor then replaces the board members with people who are friendly to the governor and the businessperson gets his permit.

Many people recognize that the Environmental Protection Agency is the greatest destroyer of jobs, businesses and rights of private property in the United States. EPA is a federal agency that was created in the early 1970s. After the law was implemented, EPA delayed allowing American industry—in particular Texas industry—to expand its facilities or even to make needed repairs or install non-polluting equipment, until EPA had issued its new rules. After a five year delay which caused substantial business interruption, loss of jobs and the resultant loss of ability of many American industries to compete with foreign nations, EPA established rules for the installation of "scrubbers" on smokestacks even though the engineering technology had been available for more than a decade. It was rumored at the time that the real reason for EPA's delay was to allow air pollution to get worse in order to enhance the public's perceived need for the then-new federal EPA agency.

EPA also had a role in the events that ultimately led to the flooding of New Orleans during Hurricane Katrina. In the 1960s, Congress had appropriated the money for the Corps of Engineers to increase the height of the levies that were protecting New Orleans; however, once EPA became established, a group of environmentalists sued the Corps and halted the project. The suit dragged on for about 30 years and the Corps gave up trying to deal with the lawsuit only a few years before Hurricane Katrina struck. The Corps wound up using the money on other projects. The hurricane resulted in hundreds of people losing their lives, multi-millions of dollars in property damage, and temporary closure of a major U.S. shipping port.

As a result of EPA's policies, not many companies can get the permits to deal with hazardous waste in the United States, even though the need for disposal of this kind of waste is acute. One businessman with a history of building up companies and employing thousands of people was able to accomplish the task, and as a result, he was able to employ a number of out-of-work Texans. Thanks to environmental regulations, however, he not only had to deal with environmental agencies, but he also had to deal with a governor with his hand out.

According to an Austin American Statesman article, "A project to bury tons of contaminated Hudson River bottom amid the rock of West Texas, seemingly biblical in its scope, could make the state one of the largest receptacles for hazardous waste in the country. Waste Control Specialists is owned by investor Harold Simmons, who was the third-largest single contributor to Gov. Rick Perry during the 2006 election cycle, donating $315,000, according to Texans for Public Justice, a nonprofit that tracks money in politics. Since 2001, Simmons' contributions to Perry have totaled more than $500,000. Last year (2008) the company got the go-ahead from the Texas Commission on Environmental Quality, whose members are appointed by the governor, to take radioactive waste at its dump site."[110]

Simmons had created Waste Control Specialists in 1995 to enter the rapidly growing market for the processing, treatment, storage, and disposal of hazardous waste materials in Texas. Money was provided for the construction of a facility in west Texas, which accepted its first waste materials for disposal in the winter of 1997. In the spring of 1997, Waste Control Specialists applied for authorization to treat, store, and dispose of low-level radioactive waste materials. All of this took place before Rick Perry became governor, yet it was 2008 when Simmons finally got his permits.

Capitalism is an economic system characterized by private or corporate ownership of capital goods, by investments that are determined by private decision, and by prices, production, and the distribution of goods that are determined mainly by competition in a free market. Capitalism and liberty originally drove the economic wealth of the nation.

The object of corporatism is to allow the corporation and government to reach an agreement whereby the government will require the consumer to pay an enforced price for a product, so that the corporation is assured it will make a guaranteed profit. Corporatism is the basis of "too big to fail," where the government protects the largest banks in the country from failure or even loss of profits. Capitalism on the other hand, contrary to corporatism, produces the best product at the cheapest price and still allows the business to make a profit by selling the product on the free market.

According to U.S. Rep. Ron Paul in *Socialism vs. Corporatism*, "Socialism is a system where the government directly owns and manages businesses…. Lately many have characterized this (Obama) administration as socialist, or having strong socialist leanings. I differ with this characterization. This is not to say Mr. Obama believes in free-markets by any means. On the contrary, he has done and said much that demonstrates his fundamental misunderstanding and hostility towards the truly free market. But a closer, honest examination of his policies and actions in office reveals that, much like the previous administration, he is very much a corporatist. This in many ways can be more insidious and worse than being an outright socialist.

"Socialism is government ownership of industry; but under corporatism, industry remains in nominally private hands. "Obama's policies increase government control of private industries and expand de facto subsidies to big businesses. Although the current system may not be pure socialism, neither is it free-market since government controls the private sector through taxes, regulations and subsidies, and has done so for decades.

"A careful examination of the policies pursued by the Obama administration and his allies in Congress shows that their agenda is corporatist. Obamacare forces every American to purchase private health insurance or pay a fine. It also includes subsidies for low-income Americans and government-run health care 'exchanges'. Large insurance and pharmaceutical companies benefit from the legislation because their profits would be guaranteed.

"President Obama's 'cap and trade' legislative attempts are actually intended to provide subsidies and special privileges to large businesses that engage in 'carbon trading.' Large corporations such as General Electric support cap-and-trade."[111]

With regard to corporatism, Governor Rick Perry's philosophy appears to be very close to the philosophy of current President Barack Obama. However, as the American voter well knows, it is very difficult for most political candidates to raise the money to campaign for, much less get elected to, any higher office without first pandering for direct or indirect donations through PAC organizations that are getting money from large international corporations and union organizations. Those corporations and organizations always expect something in return, especially special favors from government

In some cases, the Perry administration has simply given away Texas taxpayer dollars to corporations in loans and gifts. The Texas Enterprise Fund is a business incentive fund that Governor Rick Perry signed into law in 2003. The fund, which had an initial $295 million taxpayer-funded investment, was expected to be used as a recruitment tool to attract new businesses to Texas or assist with expansion of an existing business. After Texas had distributed the money to various companies, the number of actual jobs created was dismal. Twenty of the 55 companies to receive money were contributors to the Rick Perry campaign.[112] In addition, there were allegations that companies made donations to the Republican Governors' Association that in turn made campaign contributions to Perry's campaign.

Many states have established commissions that use lowered taxes to try to attract businesses to move to their state to create jobs. On January 23, 2008, reporter Mark Duncan[113] wrote that Governor Perry's Enterprise Fund is giving away money to Countrywide Financial for "literally doing nothing." Duncan wrote, "Many Texas political observers have long seen the Enterprise Fund as a corporate welfare fund, giving money away to companies that don't need it with little or no oversight of how the funds are spent." Duncan noted, "According to a business brief on January 17, 2008, 'Bank of America Mum on Job Plan,' our governor and Legislature loaned/gave California-based Countrywide Financial $20 million of taxpayer money to 'create' 7,500 new jobs … in Texas by 2010."

Countrywide then went bankrupt shortly thereafter under allegations of fraud. Countrywide later became known as a primary cause of the subprime loan mortgage meltdown. Perry's Texas Enterprise fund also gave $15 million to Washington Mutual before it was closed.

Texas public university system regents have also given close to $100,000 per regent to Perry's campaigns. In January 2009, Governor Rick Perry and two other state leaders gave the Texas A&M University System $50 million out of the Texas Enterprise Fund to build a new research facility, without seeking approval from a 17-member panel that usually advises them on such decisions.[114]

Of course, most businesspeople and individual citizens in Texas do not have the financial resources to give tens of thousands of dollars to Governor Rick Perry's campaigns. But the field of regulated businesses in Texas is wide enough for the taking, and everyone employed in a regulated business or profession that requires a state license of any kind, is vulnerable to being hit up for a contribution to the governor.

In Texas, some businesspeople in a state-government regulated businesses find they must contribute to certain candidates to keep state government off their backs. Governor Rick Perry's appointee as chairman of the Texas Alcoholic Beverage commission was caught soliciting contributions for the governor's re-election campaign from the owners of bars and restaurants he regulates. In an email to hundreds of restaurants that serve alcohol, Jose Cuevas allegedly sought donations of $1,000 to $5,000 for a Perry fundraiser at an Austin steakhouse. Cuevas, a Midland restaurateur was appointed by Perry to the commission in 2004 and was then named chairman. The agency regulates all phases of the alcoholic beverage business in Texas, including the restaurants whose owners he asked to give money.[115]

Although some physicians and engineers do give large amounts of money to Governor Perry's campaigns, and do wind up sitting on state boards and commissions (or controlling those who do), drug companies, health care companies and large homebuilding corporations are the ones that really benefit from Governor Perry's choices of people to place on the Texas Medical Board or the Texas Board of Professional Engineers. Governor Perry is a sound believer in globalism and NAFTA, and with regard to the licensed professions, his political and business philosophy is no different from that of other globalists—the cheaper the labor to provide the service, the greater the profit. To Governor Rick Perry, public safety is irrelevant.

10

❧ DOES YOUR NAFTA DOCTOR SPEAK ENGLISH? ❧

You can fool some of the people all of the time, and all of the people some of the time, but you cannot fool all of the people all of the time.

~ Abraham Lincoln (attributed)

Governor Rick Perry is using NAFTA to import into Texas those foreign fakers who have no interest in our Constitution or our freedoms, and who falsely claim to have the education and experience necessary to practice a profession.

Child labor means cheap labor, and international corporations thrive on cheap labor. According to a December 18, 2010, article in the Huffington Post: "There are some 128 goods among the products that most commonly use child labor.... The broad definition of exploitive labor by underage workers ... includes 'slavery or practices similar to slavery; the sale or trafficking of children; debt bondage or serfdom; the forcible recruitment of children for use in armed conflict; the commercial sexual exploitation of children; the involvement of children in drug trafficking; and work that is likely to harm children's health, safety, or morals.' The vast majority of the exploitive labor done by children is in agriculture (60 percent), followed by services (26 percent), and industry (7 percent)."

The reason the Clinton administration downplayed human rights abuses in the People's Republic of China in favor of supporting renewal of its most-favored-nation trade status and also supporting the admission of China into the World Trade Organization, was strictly economic.[116] International corporations required a secure economic relationship with China, which required overriding moralistic concerns for human rights.

Now thanks to NAFTA, whether or not they care to admit it, most Americans depend every day on slave labor so that they can enjoy their "American lifestyle" and buy low-cost imported goods at Wal-Mart, Target, Dicks Sporting Goods and a host of other large U.S. "box store" merchants at the cost of US jobs. According to the Huffington Post, there are a large number of countries that import products into the United States produced by slave labor including carpets, cocoa, coal, diamonds, clothes, rice, cattle, coffee, brick, tobacco, sugarcane, cotton and gold. Ultimately, those low-cost goods come at a high price that translates into lost jobs, lower wages and unsupportable U.S. trade deficits.

At one time in the not too distant past, the United States government stood on humanitarian principles against the exploitation of children and the practice of slave labor taking place anywhere in the world, especially China. Globalism, politics, and the Federal Reserve have changed all that. William Greider recounted what happened in the financial/political world during the Reagan administration in the early 1980s:

"If the recession lasted through 1982, with no sign of relief, Republicans would lose Congressional seats and possibly the majority control of the Senate. Until mid October, 1981, banks kept their basic loan rate at 19 percent, even though other short term rates had fallen substantially. The real return for bankers naturally increased. Republican attitudes toward Wall Street depended on where the Republicans were from, from the Midwest farm states and the developing provinces of the South and West or from the financial citadels in the money center cities.[117]

"Volcker knew that many of the key legislative players were on his side. Senators like Jake Garn of Utah, the Republican chairman of the Senate Banking committee, and ranking Democrat Proxmire of Wisconsin, supported what the Fed was doing and they and many others would defend the Fed against legislative assaults."[118]

And so the Federal Reserve and international corporations drove down the cost of American labor by encouraging the importation of cheap labor and goods made with slave labor. For decades, Mexico has needed money to repay its debt to the Federal Reserve and where, other than south of the border, can cheap labor be found for direct import into the United States? Mexico is a major oil exporter to the United States and apparently the money that Mexico could have spent to help its poor, has instead gone to pay interest on Mexico's debt to the Federal Reserve. As a result, the poor then go to the United States to survive.

Mexicans and South Americans are not the only ones trying to enter the United States illegally. People from the Middle East have been found to adopt Spanish-sounding or Christian names and illegally enter the United States through Mexico. Lost Korans are some of the items found in the trail of debris leading northward from the Mexican border into Arizona.

But Arizona is not the only state threatened by the influx of foreign nationals. Texas is on the front line of international corporate-based cartels of all types that are attempting to enter the United States. Austin has designated itself to be a "sanctuary city" and has also become a major US illegal-drug transportation center, where Federal immigration law is ignored and certain foreign businesses have no better friend than Austin citizen—and also Governor of Texas—Rick Perry.

Governor Rick Perry, in his effort to drive down the salaries and wages earned by Texas physicians, has implemented a plan to import low-wage, foreign physicians into the country. On May 11, 2010, the Texas Tribune wrote:[119] "Newly licensed doctors enlisting to treat the state's Medicaid and Medicare patients are more likely to have been trained at international medical schools.... Of the roughly 1,500 doctors who have received fast-tracked licenses in the last three years

84

in exchange for agreeing to treat the state's neediest patients, nearly 40 percent were trained at international medical schools, everywhere from India and Mexico to Uzbekistan and Rwanda—while a quarter were trained at Texas medical schools. The Texas Medical Board fast-tracked more licenses for doctors trained in Pakistan than it did for those educated in Louisiana or Oklahoma."

No other country is known for having top-rated medical training facilities like those that are found in the U.S., and the inevitable result will be low quality primary care for the state's most needy citizens. The downgrading of medical quality in Texas is due to Perry's efforts to implement NAFTA in professional services in Texas.

In 1988, Canada and the United States signed the Canada-United States Free Trade Agreement, with the express purpose of expanding trade blocs such as the Maastricht Treaty which created the European Union in 1992. President Bill Clinton signed the trade agreement on December 8, 1993.

The governments of Canada, Mexico and the United States implemented the North American Free Trade Agreement, or NAFTA, on January 1, 1994. Many Americans are now convinced that the real reason they do not have jobs right now is due to the implementation of NAFTA, with its resulting international price fixing and low quality imports. Many Americans—those who do have jobs—find themselves having to work at low wages in order to compete with government subsidized slave-wage labor rates paid in foreign countries such as China.

Most American are also convinced that, as a result of NAFTA, corporate stockholders, executives, and Wall Street investors are the ones who are making all the money; with the corporations using accounting gimmicks to park their revenues overseas to reduce their U.S. tax burden. Most Americans now want NAFTA renegotiated or abolished entirely.[120]

A special trade category was included in NAFTA that would permit replacement of America's trained professionals with low cost, unqualified foreign doctors. A trade category called "TN (Trade NAFTA) status" is a special non-immigrant status in the United States unique to citizens of Canada and Mexico. TN status permits U.S.,

Canadian and Mexican citizens the opportunity to work in each other's countries in the practice of certain professional occupations such as accounting, architecture, computer systems, dentistry, engineering, geology, law and medicine.

The TN status bears a similarity, in some ways, to the H-1B visa. Within the TN set of occupations, a Canadian or Mexican national can work for up to three years at a time within the United States. According to NAFTA, the TN status may be renewed indefinitely in three-year increments, although it is not intended to be a permanent visa.

Most states in the United States are believed to have resisted international efforts to expand trade in the professions. America's ethical and technical training in the professions is superior to all other countries, and American citizens prefer that physicians, engineers, and others who obligate themselves to protect the public health, safety and welfare, are properly trained, have sufficient experience, and pass professional examinations before becoming licensed.

However, in Rick Perry's Texas, NAFTA in the professions has expanded to allow people from almost all other countries worldwide to gain a shortcut to practice a profession with a professional license. Governor Perry has brought this about with his appointments to the state boards, agencies and commissions that now write rules that violate the U.S. and Texas constitutional protections that Americans enjoy. Perry's appointees now allow foreign nationals to gain a "path to practice," regardless of qualifications or commitment to public safety, by issuing provisional licenses. As a result, the elderly in Texas—especially the poor, but also others regardless of income—are particularly vulnerable.

The purpose of NAFTA is for the various participating governments to control the price of labor in their own countries so that the goods sold to other countries guarantee international corporations a profit. The cheaper the price of the labor to make the product, the greater the profit. The quality of the final product is irrelevant. Only the lowest price matters.

A significant element of Perry's platform in Texas has been "tort reform"—or as Governor Perry says, "over-suing"—which actually has resulted in the near abolition of a medically injured person's constitutional rights to trial by jury.

In 2003, Governor Perry sponsored a controversial state constitutional amendment that benefitted drug companies, insurance corporations, and hospitals. The amendment put a cap on medical malpractice awards, a proposal that was narrowly approved by voters. In doing this, Perry began to open a path to practice to the worst kinds of doctors to treat Texans—the people who, as medical practitioners, now have nothing to fear financially from their mistakes. At Perry's insistence the medical cap was set so low that lawyers could not make any money helping people who had been critically injured by their health care providers; so lawyers refused to accept so-called "med-mal" cases. Almost overnight, it became nearly impossible for medically-injured patients to obtain redress in the courts because they could not find a lawyer willing to take on their case. Incompetent doctors who had been sued in other states then moved to Texas and opened up shop.

The results have been dramatic, with a general decline in attention to safety. Recently a large Dallas hospital warned patients that it had discovered that the instruments used in gynecology had not been sterilized. At another Texas hospital, a patient was told she had cancer and only a few weeks to live. When the doctors performed a biopsy they accidently punctured her lung, but discovered that she did not have cancer after all. All she can hope for, if she survives, is that the doctors can patch her up well enough to send her home.

Meanwhile, the competent doctors in Texas began to suffer with Perry's selection of medical board members. In 2002, Governor Perry appointed Dr. Roberta Kalafut to the Texas Medical Board. Dr. Kalafut became president of the medical board in 2005. She was subsequently accused by a doctor's organization of abusing her authority. She later resigned her position. Jane Orient, executive director of the Association of American Physicians and Surgeons which filed a lawsuit against Kalafut and other members of the board, said "We applaud Kalafut's resignation. AAPS has received far more complaints from good physicians in Texas about their medical board than from any other state." The suit included allegations that the board was engaging in manipulation of anonymous complaints; conflicts of interest; violation of due process; breach of privacy; retaliation against those who speak out and misusing its authority.[121] [122]

The Travis County District Attorney was also asked to investigate charges that a doctor, whose wife served on the medical board, had filed anonymous complaints against competitors and that the wife had used her position of authority at the board to assure that disciplinary action was taken against her husband's competitors. It was reported that this would appear to violate Section 39.03 of the Texas Penal Code relating to abuse of power, as well as the federal anti-racketeering act (RICO).[123]

In 2007, a physician who wished to remain anonymous wrote (edited): "Fear and terror are shaping the medical practice in this country everywhere. It doesn't take much to destroy the livelihood of a doctor. Doctors are silenced everywhere. Slaving doctors is the new form of slavery that appeared in USA beginning in 1986. In 1986, the U.S. Congress introduced the Healthcare Quality Improvement Act (HCQIA) that gave an absolute power to a few doctors. This law destroyed the integrity of medical practice everywhere. This law allows a few doctors who are able to achieve power in the hospitals and on the medical boards to control the majority of doctors. This law prevents the victim-doctor from going to a civil court to protect his civil rights no matter how severe the civil rights violations are. Does power corrupt? The answer is yes. Do those who are corrupt lust for power? The answer is also yes…. Silencing doctors at the hospital level and at the medical board level has prevented doctors from reporting serious errors and has made doctors ineffective members of the healthcare team."

Another anonymous physician wrote: "The Medical Licensing Boards are rubber stamps for the self-styled lawyer prosecutor. The Board is a front organization for yet another lawyer operation to take over health care…. The result is a long series of lawyer gotchas on trivial regulatory deviations. Meanwhile, highly dangerous doctors who are total threats to patient survival, go unmolested by the paper shuffling, lazy, incompetent threats to clinical care."

The poor and the elderly in Texas will be the first to suffer from

Governor Rick Perry's form of tort reform and health care. The Texas Tribune wrote: "Doctors trained outside the U.S. or Canada already make up more than a fifth of the state's licensed physicians and more than a quarter of the new doctors licensed every year.... As more longtime doctors stop seeing money-losing Medicaid and Medicare patients—the result of far-from-adequate federal and state reimbursement rates—the burden will increasingly fall to these international medical school graduates. Many of them have visas that are contingent upon their work with poor and underinsured populations in cities and small towns. With health care reform expected to push an estimated 1 million new Texans onto state Medicaid rolls, the pressure on the doctors who do accept these patients will only mount.... Agreeing to treat Medicaid and Medicare patients, or to practice in an underserved community, is also a fast way to build a practice and build credibility."[124]

But to reflect the kinds of doctors that are being imported into Texas, the article notes: "These doctors vary in their success—and sometimes the cultural barriers they face are insurmountable. In one case, a Middle Eastern doctor came to practice at a federally-financed clinic, only to realize the facility's executive director was female. He left, saying that in his country, 'men didn't take orders from women'."

At present, the only solution seems to be: If you are female and living in Texas, get medical referrals from established physicians, stay out of the hospital if you can, and watch out for foreign-trained Medicare and Medicaid doctors. In Midland an elderly woman was treated by a Texas-licensed Pakistani physician who evidently knew very little about proper care, so he wrote prescriptions for several different drugs for her to take at the same time. The woman had a severe reaction but another physician took her off the medications. A few months later the physician fled the country for Pakistan before the FBI could arrest him. It was reported that for years he had been deeply involved in Medicare fraud and was over-billing Medicare as if he had been working an average of 36 hours each day, 7 days a week. The government had kept paying his fraudulent bills. His records indicated that he had also been billing for patients who did not even exist.

The new healthcare law will pack 32 million newly insured people into emergency rooms already crammed beyond capacity.[125] According to the Houston Chronicle:[126] "Texas doctors are opting out of Medicare at alarming rates, frustrated by reimbursement cuts they say make participation in government-funded care of seniors unaffordable.... New data shows 100 to 200 Texas doctors a year are now ending all involvement with the Medicare program.... The opt-outs follow years of declining Medicare reimbursement that culminated in a looming 21 percent cut in 2010. Congress has voted three times to postpone the cut. Now, more than four in 10 doctors are considering the move."

Recently, Governor Rick Perry increased his crackdown on the constitutional rights of Texas doctors with his medical board. When any professional is accused of a violation of rule or law, he or she is normally afforded the constitutional rights of due process, including a hearing before a judge. During the recent Texas Legislative session, a bill was introduced to address how the Texas Medical Board delegates the disposition of contested case hearings to the State Office of Administrative Hearings. Governor Rick Perry then vetoed the bill saying he "felt that the board should have the final decision authority on sanctions against doctors, not an administrative law judge."[127]

Most recently, to add insult to injury, the Perry-appointed regents to the University of Texas System have decided to start a program that cuts back on the number of credit hours students need to receive in order to graduate with a medical degree.[128] This will inevitably result in a lowered world view by the students, and a lower quality of medical care in Texas. Theoretically, hospitals will be able to hire them as pill-pushing technocrats for less money, and Medicare will also pay them less than their more qualified counterparts. The UT program prompted a letter to the Austin American Statesman that read: "Now the University of Texas System proposes a plan to shorten the time it takes to becoming a medical doctor. So our future Texas doctors will have gotten grades they didn't really earn in a shorter amount of time?"[129]

Drug companies appear to be behind the push to get competent doctors out of the way, in order to allow foreign technocrats to practice medicine in Texas—the ones who prescribe drugs the drug companies tell them to prescribe. Doctors are familiar with hordes of salespeople from drug companies that try to get the doctor to try out a new drug on their patients. For the safety of the patients, some doctors do everything to avoid prescribing certain drugs at all.

Almost every hour of the day, every day of the week, the American television viewer is subjected to drug advertisements. There are very qualified doctors in Texas who refuse to prescribe many of the drugs that people see advertised on television because of the drug's life-threatening side effects. If the doctor won't prescribe the drugs, the drug companies don't make the large profits needed to benefit their stockholders and advertise on television as much as they do.

A person watches the advertisement on television and, thinking the drug will provide the cure, will then ask the doctor to prescribe the advertised drug. The reputable doctor, fearful of the potential adverse consequences for the patient, refuses to prescribe the drug. The patient then goes down the street to a doctor who lacks the education or morals necessary to know whether or not the drug should be prescribed, and that doctor then prescribes the drug. The patient takes the drug and possibly develops adverse side effects or dies. A vicious cycle encompasses the doctor and the patient alike.

One way for a drug company to make a profit under Rick Perry's corporatist-based system is to reach an agreement with government that forces a certain portion of the population to take the drug. Drug experimentation on human beings is illegal in the United States, but if some people die from using the drug then the drug manufacturer can defend itself by telling a court that the government ordered the drug to be administered. The estates of the deceased people have no recourse against the government, and thanks to Governor Perry's version of tort reform having passed in the Texas Legislature, the estates have little recourse against the drug company, the hospital, or the physician who prescribed the drug. The scenario is a guaranteed "win" in Texas for drug companies.

In 2007, Governor Rick Perry signed an executive order mandating that Texas schoolgirls in the sixth grade be required to subject themselves to vaccination against human papillomavirus, or HPV, a sexually transmitted virus that can result in cervical cancer.

Merck & Co. manufactures the drug, and Rick Perry's ties with Merck run deep.[130] Amid a public outcry, Texas legislators eventually overturned Perry's order.

In a recent Austin American Statesman article,[131] Mr. Javin Browder was quoted as saying, "(Governor Perry's executive order) was a pretty extreme instance in which he abused his executive authority." Browder is evidently a Tea Party supporter leading an effort to draft U.S. Sen. Jim DeMint to run for president, saying the Republican establishment's support of Perry makes him wary of the Texas governor. Browder also said that Tea Party supporters have told him that Perry has used the Tea Party when it is politically expedient. He said, "He's played up to them a lot to get a power base," according to the article.

Governor Perry had issued his executive order at a time that Merck was bankrolling efforts to pass laws in state legislatures throughout the country, mandating that girls as young as 11 or 12 be vaccinated with its product. Reportedly, Merck had doubled its lobbying budget in Texas and had funneled money through Women in Government, an advocacy group. According to an Associate Press article and KBTX.com, Perry had several ties to Merck and Women in Government. One of the drug company's three lobbyists in Texas was Mike Toomey, his former chief of staff. His current chief of staff's mother-in-law, Texas Republican state Rep. Dianne White Delisi, was reported to be a state director for Women in Government.[132]

Mike Toomey has recently formed the Super PAC "Make Us Great Again." According to an article in the Huffington Post, "Toomey is so close to the Perry inner circle he even co-owns a private island in New Hampshire with Perry's campaign manager Dave Carney. Toomey was also listed in a Texas Tribune report on the 'folks' behind Perry."[133]

Also, according to the Huffington Post article,[134] "Another (Super PAC) committee, 'Americans for Rick Perry,' is run by California political consultant Bob Schuman, a former campaign consultant for former Sen. Phil Gramm (R-Texas), Perry's political mentor. Schuman's consulting firm has also represented the pharmaceutical company Merck."

Some have said that the decades-long War on Drugs is actually a war on the growing and sale of medical marijuana; and the drug companies knew long ago that marijuana would provide the same relief from pain as most pain-killers that could be developed in pharmaceutical laboratories, but also knew the marijuana would not be as dangerous. As the argument goes, the War on Drugs is really an agreement between government and the drug industry to keep a drug—medical marijuana—off the market and allow the drug industry to monopolize the pain-killer market with a guaranteed profit.

Several states have tried to legalize medical marijuana, but the drug companies appear to be fighting the effort in the legislatures and the courts. A recent decision by a Michigan appeals court said, "the 2008 medical marijuana law, as well as the state health code, doesn't let people sell pot to each other, even if they're among the 99,500 who have state-issued marijuana cards."[135]

Corporatists are monopolists and monopolists hate competition.

11

❧ BUILDINGS AND BRIDGES DON'T SIMPLY FALL DOWN ❦

There's going to be an event, Aaron, and out of that event you're going to see ... we are going to go into Afghanistan so we can run pipelines from the Caspian Sea. We're going to go into Iraq to take the oil and establish a base in the Middle East.

~ Nicholas Rockefeller, during a conversation with filmmaker Aaron Russo, eleven months before 9/11

The television images of New York's World Trade Center twin towers buildings collapsing on 9/11 with people still inside traumatized the nation and much of the rest of the civilized world. Shortly thereafter, it was said that even Osama bin Laden had been surprised that the buildings had collapsed; but the visual images were indeed enough to project the terrorist's impact into the American psyche and economy. The aftermath of the attacks that resulted in Congress passing the Patriot Act, had a devastating effect on the Constitutional freedoms that had been enjoyed by individual Americans before that day; and also displayed the statist ideals of many of the nation's public officials.

The buildings had been constructed in the early 1970s. In the years since 9/11, structural engineers have contended that one reason the buildings collapsed from the ensuing fire was that the original design engineers had included an insufficient number of structural steel horizontal I-beams at each floor level. These beams are required to connect the buildings' perimeter steel columns to the central core. The design engineers had instead used cheaper light-weight steel "bar-joists" to provide some degree of stability although it is well known to engineers that fire quickly causes non-fire-protected steel bar joists to buckle and pull apart at their connections.

In addition, the building's design engineers had not utilized the latest engineering principles related to prevention of "progressive collapse" that were only then being developed in Europe, and were being recommended by the American Society of Civil Engineers. The standards had not been incorporated into U.S. building codes, and because of the additional cost to building owners, most of these standards are still not incorporated into building codes that are in use today. Incorporating those engineering principles into the original design of the buildings at the World Trade Center would have increased the amount of required structural steel within the buildings and would have cost the building owners more money.

Greed was a significant factor in the engineering design of the buildings. The engineers were prevented from using proper building column spacing grid layouts because the owners wanted to maximize the amount of leasable office space, by eliminating interior columns as much as possible. The engineers were told to place the columns at the exterior perimeter of the building and at the building core, but not in the office areas. In normal office buildings, the floor area of each individual column in an office area cannot be considered "leasable floor area" and no rentals can be obtained from those relatively-small areas.

Middle-Eastern terrorists with computers, structural engineering software and access to the engineering plans, plus a little engineering design knowledge, can (and probably did) figure out which part of the buildings to strike with airplanes in order to inflict the maximum amount of damage. Now terrorists of all sorts, whether they are foreign or domestic, realize that to attack the nation's infrastructure, all they need is access to software and the engineering plans.

Even though bin Laden is dead, others of his murderous ilk remain. The Navy SEAL raid that took down Osama bin Laden produced a cache of electronic and handwritten materials outlining al-Qaeda plots to attack infrastructure targets in the US, such as water supplies, transportation systems and dams.[136] One of al-Qaeda's goals is to poison US water supplies.

While Americans stand in line at airports waiting to subject themselves to all kinds of personal indignities simply because they want to travel somewhere, the nation's enemies are slipping into the nation through the back door. Governor Rick Perry's administration has not only compromised the credibility of the Texas Medical Board, but has also compromised the credibility of another state agency—the Texas Board of Professional Engineers.

Governor Perry has implemented a NAFTA "path to practice" that grants foreign engineers a professional engineering license to practice in Texas without taking the engineering licensing exams. With the anticipated influx of foreign engineers into Texas, the state's and the nation's existing and planned infrastructure—including highways and bridges, chemical plants, water treatment plants, and federal and state facilities—is rapidly becoming vulnerable to international terrorism.

Terrorists with limited engineering knowledge but who have access to a computer, can gain enough fundamental knowledge of structural and electrical engineering to determine how to design a "weak link" into an American public works project. Thanks in large part to NAFTA, foreign engineers do not even have to have a physical presence on American soil in order to design projects to be constructed in the United States. They can have a consortium of foreign engineers do the design through a globalist engineering corporation. Most importantly, Governor Perry's efforts will insure that the foreign engineers are actually present on American soil.

Proper engineering education is almost nonexistent in most foreign countries and, as a result, people are simply "registered" in their countries as engineers instead of "licensed" as they are in the United States. Being licensed in the United States requires passing a rigid series of professional engineering examinations that most foreign individuals are unable to pass. Nevertheless, the foreign engineers title themselves "engineers" in their own countries even though in the United States they would be considered incompetent in the practice of engineering.

When an engineering firm is given a contract to design a public project that is to be built in the United States, most city and state agencies look for only one professional engineering seal on the drawings. If the plans are prepared by an international engineering corporation with hundreds of "engineers" but are sealed by only one engineer licensed in the state where the project will be undertaken, then the project will be approved for permit, no matter how many foreign, untrained "engineer-fakers" are actually involved in the actual preparation of the plans.

Since most foreign engineers are not really engineers in the true sense of the word, they form consortiums with one or more American engineers who do some minor amount of work on the project and then place their PE seals on the plans. These types of American engineers are held in low esteem in the profession; but the state engineering boards, particularly in Texas, are unwilling to stop them.

To illustrate the procedure, a Texas engineer received a telephone call from a person involved with an international consortium a few weeks after 9/11. The telephone conversation was recalled by the engineer in the following manner, with names changed:

"Hello, Mr. Notsogullible, PE," said the voice on the other end of the line. "I represent Yahaba-Alababa Engineering Outsourcing Corporation and we would like to offer you a deal where you can make a lot of money. We have reached an agreement with an American government official to provide engineering services for an addition to a courthouse building, and we need an American licensed professional engineer to team up with.

"Here is how it works: We work with American officials to get an American engineering project going our way, and then our people do all of the engineering design and CAD drafting work here in Dubai. We have the project now and your government has agreed to pay us a $300,000 fee to do the engineering design of the building under a NAFTA minority procurement contract. Our labor costs are rock bottom and we can do all the engineering and drawings for you on our CAD computers for $50,000. When we're done, we will send the drawings to you and then you put your Professional Engineering seal on the drawings so that the client can get a building permit. You don't need to do anything else. We keep $50,000 of the fee and give you the remaining $250,000 for stamping the drawings with your seal and representing yourself as the Engineer of Record. There's more about what we do on our website."

Mr. Notsogullible, PE said "Sounds like you are a NAFTA guy. I guess big business deals are made with your kind all the time. It sounds like your so-called engineers aren't educated at all, and if they are educated, they probably went to school at Al Qaeda U. They probably don't really know anything about real engineering. Thanks to people like you, I can't even find a decent bicycle tire pump at Target—it's junk made in China with no engineering or manufacturing skills whatsoever.

"I'll bet," Mr. Notsogullible continued, "the only thing your guys know about engineering is how to run software on a computer, and make bombs. Your guys are obviously not qualified to get a professional license if they are willing to take only $50,000 to get a foot in the door on a project like you described. I think the real reason for your phone call is to try to get me on board to make your project look legitimate."

The phone went "click" on the other end of the line and the caller's website disappeared from the Internet shortly after that.

An example of the type of drinking-water threat to Texas citizens by foreign engineers who are located in other countries is a new water treatment plant called WTP4 that is currently under construction along the shores of Lake Travis above Mansfield Dam, near Austin. The primary source of water in Austin is Lake Austin, and water from Lake

Travis flows through Mansfield Dam into Lake Austin.

The WTP4 plant was recently designed by a consortium of engineering firms with at least two of those firms having offices in the Middle East. A local reputable engineering firm with American engineers is also involved, most likely because the firm is known to City of Austin officials who permitted the project.

Austin is the capital city and seat of government of Texas, and also home to the University of Texas and many research centers. On any given day, there are approximately one million people living in and traveling into and out of the Austin area. When the state legislature is in session, people travel from all over Texas and elsewhere to lobby and observe their legislators in action. With Austin's extreme left-wing political ideology, particularly within the politically active inner-city core that elects almost all members of the city council, every effort is made to award city contracts in the name of "multiculturalism." Historically when money is spread around the right way, "fairness" trumps qualifications any day of the week in Austin.

The new water treatment plant WTP4 will consist of water intakes, a pump station, and pipelines that will carry water from Lake Travis into the treatment facility. Transmission mains will then carry water from the treatment plant and then into the water distribution system and eventually into homes, schools, fire hydrants and businesses in the growing area north and northwest of Austin. The first phase of the plant will produce 50 million gallons of water a day and will be operational by 2014. The plant, after all the phases are built, will ultimately be able to produce an additional 6 times as much fresh water (300 mgd) as it will produce during its initial phase.

In late 2010, after reviewing the plans for WTP4 and with the construction of the plant already underway, the president of an Austin engineering firm warned City of Austin officials that there were engineering deficiencies in the plans and specifications prepared for the project by the international engineers. The Austin engineer noted that significant parts of the project did not appear to be properly engineered. Specifically, there is only one large water intake from the lake to the plant, and that intake is located adjacent to the bottom of the lake. The water intake consists of a long length of thin wall steel piping, nine feet in diameter and fully exposed on all sides of the pipe, instead of a series of short pipes encased in concrete near the bottom of the lake.

American engineers are well aware of the importance of protective design when they design infrastructure projects. Foreign engineers either don't know or don't care about protecting the lives of Americans. In the case of Austin's WTP4, the water intake pipe has not been designed to thwart a terrorist attack. In fact, the design actually encourages a terrorist wearing scuba gear to find an isolated location in the lake along the pipe, and then plant an underwater explosive / biological-chemical device. Once the device is detonated, the biological-chemical element would poison the water that would pass through the plant and reach the homes and businesses of hundreds of thousands of people in the Austin area. The explosion would also draw in large quantities of rocks and debris off the bottom of the lake into the pumps before the pumps could be shut off, potentially shutting down the entire plant for an extended period of time, damaging the electrical circuitry, and dumping chemicals back into Lake Travis.

The engineering design, with the plans evidently in the hands of a foreign government or foreign entity such as al-Qaeda, has the potential to result in environmental havoc in Lake Travis at a critical location near Mansfield Dam. In the letter, the engineer blamed the City of Austin for having people in the Middle East design the new Austin water treatment plant with those people potentially selling those plans to persons who do not view America in a positive light. The engineer noted that the "City of Austin taxpayers have already paid in excess of $1 million to the engineers who designed the plant," and recommended a criminal investigation of those involved. The engineer also recommended redesign of the water intake along with specialized analysis and possible redesign of the entire water treatment plant. To date, no known changes have been made in the engineering design of the plant, although there has recently been a move by Austin citizens to stop the construction of the plant entirely.

Water treatment plants are not the only type of American infrastructure that al-Qaeda is interested in destroying. Bridges are also targets, and it is highly possible that the collapse of the Interstate 35 Bridge in Minneapolis, Minnesota was actually an act of terrorism.

On August 1, 2007, a significant portion of the 1,907 foot long Interstate 35 bridge collapsed into the Mississippi River during evening rush hour traffic. A highway repaving project had been underway. Thirteen people died and 145 people were injured as spilled vehicles heaped on top of each other and spilled into the river while the roadway and its supports fell.

Recently,[137] President Obama mentioned the collapse and stated "Our roads, our bridges, and our sewer systems are deteriorating." Mr. Obama also blamed the failure of the country to restore the physical infrastructure that has resulting from "insufficient federal spending on transportation." Most Americans would agree with President Obama on this point. However, what Mr. Obama failed to mention during his speech (probably because he did not know) was the fact that deterioration was not a factor that contributed to the bridge collapse.

The engineering firm in charge of the pavement repair project would have conducted a structural analysis of the bridge months before the project began and months before the collapse. It is evident that the analysis was incorrectly performed and whoever did the analysis was incompetent or possibly a terrorist.

The engineering firm involved was an international engineering consortium that apparently employs foreign technicians as "engineers." The names and qualifications of the "engineers"—those individuals who were directly involved in the failed engineering analysis and resulting collapse of the bridge—remains unknown.

The $9 million overlay project had been underway for several weeks. On the day of the collapse, a road contractor had been adding another layer of pavement to the bridge. According to *Engineering News Record*,[138]the contractor had already finished repairing four lanes of deck and was in the process of fixing the other four when the bridge span fell. Workers were preparing to place pavement material in the southbound lanes of the highway, and piles of sand and gravel along with repaving equipment had been staged on the southern side of the bridge near the river's west bank. The National Transportation Safety Board later noted that the weight of the "staging of materials, equipment and people on the bridge may have contributed to its failure."

A problem facing the forensic engineers examining the cause of the collapse was how to explain why the collapse had occurred so long after the bridge was initially designed and constructed and after it had carried millions of vehicles. The bridge had stood 40 years before failing. Yet deterioration was not the cause of failure. The engineers discounted corrosion, weld fatigue, and rivet failure, and instead concentrated on the fact that the steel connector plates—pieces of sheet steel that are used to connect the various structural steel members together—had failed under load. Engineering analysis performed by the forensic engineers eventually showed that the connector plates, which for this particular bridge varied from ½ inch to ¾ inches thick, were too small at one or two critical locations within the bridge and they ultimately broke.

Further review showed that there had been several repaving projects over the years, and the added weight of the various layers had accumulated through the years. Thus all of the connector plates in the bridge, which had been designed to connect members carrying 1960s vintage cars and trucks—the design standard at the time—had become more and more overstressed through each addition of load during each preceding repaving project. Finally, during the most recent repaving project, when the added materials and equipment were placed on the south side lanes, the extra loads combined with the weight of the repaving equipment and materials, combined with the high load of the vehicles during rush hour traffic, were enough to fracture the smallest connector plates, disconnect the structural members from each other, and result in the collapse of the bridge.

According to *Engineering News Record*, the bridge had been designed by the engineering firm of Sverdrup & Parcel and had been opened to traffic in 1967. In 1999, Jacobs Engineering Group, Inc. of Pasadena, California had bought Sverdrup Corp. But, in analyzing the collapse, the question would have arisen among the forensic engineers and the lawyers as to how either Sverdrup or Jacobs could be held legally responsible since the addition of loads over the years that would overstress the connector plates would be unforeseen to the original bridge designers.

The engineering firm that had consulted on the repaving project was determined to be San Francisco-based URS Corporation. The engineering firm was sued by more than 100 people. On August 24, 2010 the *Wall Street Journal* and other publications announced that URS had agreed to pay $52.4 million to settle litigation brought by the victims. According to the WSJ, "URS had argued that its engineers didn't know about a design flaw in the bridge that made it vulnerable."[139]

When an engineering firm is given a bridge repaving or rehabilitation project in the United States, the firm's engineers are required to be licensed and are required to determine the entire history of the bridge to prevent failure of the bridge resulting from the project. The history is very important because it tells the engineer how the bridge has been subjected to increased dead load weights over time by repaving projects. Once the history of accumulated loads is determined, the engineer can tell if critical points of the bridge will be overstressed by the upcoming repaving project, by using a structural stress analysis to determine which particular connector plates might become overstressed by the additional loads from the new layer of pavement. In addition, before completing their analysis, the engineers are required to inspect every component of the bridge including beams, columns, braces and connector plates, especially the ones that the analysis show to be critical under the assumed loads.

American engineers are trained to know how to properly undertake these tasks. There is now substantial suspicion that URS's engineers either did not check what they were supposed to check, or did not know what they were supposed to know, reflecting the potential incompetence of the individual engineers involved.

There is also another possibility not mentioned in the news media: Could the collapse have been the result of a terrorist act? Structural engineers know that checking connector plates for the added loads from bridge repairs is basic and routine practice. The question arises: what if a foreign engineer working for a large international engineering firm did indeed undertake a structural analysis? And while doing the analysis, what if the engineer had determined that there was indeed a

103

danger from overload during the repaving work? What if the engineer reported the condition to others in the Middle East, such as al-Qaeda, a terrorist organization that would be interested in causing economic damage to the United States, by severing a vital east-west transportation economic link—a bridge across the Mississippi River? Then what if the foreign engineer then lied to his employer that there were no problems associated with the connector plates, and therefore ultimately allowed the bridge to collapse?

It is presently unknown if the engineers employed by URS who were involved in the engineering analysis were American engineers, licensed in Minnesota to protect the health, safety and welfare of the general public; or if they were like the foreign engineer-fakers being admitted into Rick Perry's Texas. In the August 23, 2010 "Statement of Settlement of I-35W Bridge Litigation", URS told its investors:[140]

"The I-35W bridge collapse was a tragedy, which the National Transportation Safety Board concluded was caused by a design flaw, compounded by large weight increases from upgrade projects over the years and the traffic and construction loads on the day the bridge collapsed. URS was not involved in the design or building of the bridge, nor was it involved in any of the later construction work, including the resurfacing work being done when the bridge collapsed.... The settlement amount of $52.4 million will be paid in full by the company's insurers."

The statement also said, "URS Corporation ... is a leading provider of engineering, construction and technical services for public agencies and private sector companies around the world.... Headquartered in San Francisco, URS Corporation has approximately 41,000 employees in a network of offices in more than 30 countries."

So what number of foreign engineers make up the 41,000 people employed by URS and what are their credentials? According to World Bank and African Union surveys, corruption costs Africa $148 billion a year and also results in a 20-30 percent cost of goods and services. Worldwide, the volume of bribes exchanging hands through public sector procurement is estimated to be $200 billion to $300 billion.[141] Bribing a public official for credentials is certainly not unheard of.

Left unsaid in the URS report could have been a missive expressing the general attitude of some globalist engineering corporations and building contractors that American professional engineers have had experience with: "The other guys are to blame—not us. Sorry, we might have screwed up but we've got enough insurance to cover our engineers' behinds—the ones who might or might not have been foreigners and might or might not have enough education to have been licensed as professional engineers to protect the health, safety and welfare of the public; so let's just move on and get back to making money for our investors. After all, large corporations are exempt from the Engineering Practices Acts in most states of the US and besides, we're the gorilla in the room and we've got friends in Washington."

The URS-investor-story does not seem to jibe with the argument that their lawyers evidently presented to the court. As previously noted, the *Wall Street Journal* stated "URS had argued that its engineers didn't know about a design flaw in the bridge that made it vulnerable." So just what was it that the engineers were doing on this project that made URS's insurers so worried about the outcome before a jury—so worried that the insurers were willing to pay out $52.4 million to settle the matter before it could go to trial?

Evidently sealed in the matter is which particular engineers were employed to analyze the structural members and also analyze the ultimately failed connectors before the repaving project began. And of even greater interest, why would the defendants want to keep unreported the names and nationalities of the engineers who failed to do their jobs correctly? And also, why keep quiet the names of the American politicians who might have granted URS the project to begin with?

* * *

In Texas, foreign engineering "fakers" no longer have to undertake their engineering design projects from afar. Now Governor Perry has implemented a NAFTA "path to practice" for foreign engineers in order to satisfy international corporations. When it comes to the willing acceptance of international corporate control of a United States public official, there is no known equal to Governor Rick Perry. Any presidential candidate who is willing to accept control by moneyed elites and globalists is unsuitable as a candidate for the highest office in the nation.

Mr. Perry's Texas Board of Professional Engineers has now established the procedure that degrades the title "professional engineer" and thereby permits marginally trained and dangerous foreign technicians to enter the country and undermine the protections to the public that professional engineering licensure affords the citizens in all of the United States. The United States government, the Federal Reserve, and large corporations have used NAFTA for years as an excuse to eliminate jobs and drive down labor costs in the United States. Now NAFTA is being used against the American professional engineers.

The Texas Board of Professional Engineers (TBPE) is a state agency established in 1937 to protect the public from unscrupulous, incompetent, and dangerous engineers. Every state has a similar board to protect the public.

Throughout his over 10 years as governor of Texas, Rick Perry has replaced or reappointed all of the Texas engineering board to fit his wishes; and now the engineering board is writing rules to establish Perry's "path to practice." This "path" will eventually allow thousands of foreign individuals with questionable backgrounds into the United States. There is minimal evidence that any of the proposed licensees have met any of the requirements to be licensed as professional engineers in any state of the United States.

By law, professional engineers are licensed to protect the public health, safety, and welfare. According to the law, "The state legislature intends that the privilege of practicing engineering be entrusted only to a person licensed and practicing under the law, and that only a person licensed under the law may engage in the practice of engineering and be represented in any way as any kind of 'engineer'; or make any professional use of the term 'engineer'."[142]

An "engineer" practicing in the United States is considered to be a professional practitioner of engineering who applies scientific knowledge, mathematics, physics, knowledge of materials, art, and ingenuity to develop solutions to technical problems. Engineers design and analyze physical systems, materials, structures, machines, and processes while considering limitations imposed by practicality, safety, and cost. Engineers are grounded in the applied sciences as distinguished from scientists who perform basic research. The work of engineers forms the link between scientific discoveries and the applications that meet the needs of society.

"Professional engineers" are those persons regulated and licensed by the state who have met higher qualification requirements than persons employed in exempt industries where meeting academic, experience, and examination requirements might not be required. State legislatures recognize the vital impact that the rapid advancement of knowledge of the mathematical, physical, and engineering sciences as applied in the practice of engineering has on the lives, property, economy, safety, and security of state residents and the national defense, and therefore licensing is used to separate the qualified from the unqualified. For similar reasons, the states also license physicians and other professionals.

In most, if not all, states a person who holds himself or herself out as a professional engineer must have graduated from an accredited engineering college or university; obtained four to five years of experience; and passed a rigorous two day set of examinations administered by the National Council of Engineering Examiners and Surveyors (NCEES). Most graduates of engineering schools who are unwilling to take (or unable to pass) the examinations, are not licensed as professional engineers. Instead, many engineering graduates go to work for government or industry, which are considered to be employers "exempt" from state licensing laws.

Persons who are not titled "professional engineer" may not use the term "engineer" in any context or setting where the public might be harmed. The "public", for instance, includes the employees who worked on the Deepwater Horizon drilling rig that exploded and sank in 2010 and it is presently unknown, but doubtful, if any of the parties involved in the design of the relevant rig and drilling components were licensed professional engineers.

The National Council of Engineering Examiners and Surveyors (NCEES) is an organization composed of all engineering and surveying licensing boards in the United States and several territories. NCEES develops, scores, and, for many states, administers examinations used for engineering licensure. The passage of NAFTA opened up a dangerous path that allowed unqualified individuals who call themselves "engineers" to enter the United States and endanger the public. The only forces capable of blocking the incompetent foreign individual are the individual state engineering practice laws and the rigid examinations promulgated by NCEES.

International corporations employ marginally trained persons who lack basic engineering and social skills, lack proper schooling, lack adequate experience, and fail to qualify to take or pass the two professional engineering examinations administered by NCEES. For decades, national and international industries have attempted to enable these types of persons to enter the United States and be titled by the states as "engineer" or "professional engineer" in an effort to lower American engineering labor costs and forego any harm to the public these actions might bring.

The American government's involvement in this nefarious activity, mainly through NAFTA, is one of the fundamental reasons that the average age of professional engineers in the United States is in the fifties and rising, and also why it is so difficult to entice young Americans to become educated as engineers. Nationwide efforts to attract young people to enter the engineering profession have centered on the need for more math and science in primary education, but have ignored the severe damage that NAFTA has caused to the workers of this nation, and is now causing the professions.

Toward the end of George W. Bush's gubernatorial administration in Texas, the Texas Board of Professional Engineers (TBPE) began to find itself subjected to pressure by international corporations to license unqualified foreign nationals as "professional engineers." The effort had begun in 1998 with an effort to license software developers as professional engineers without the applicants having taken the

NCEES-administered examinations.

To the globalists, beginning with George W. Bush as governor, Texas had become the politically vulnerable state that might allow for globalist expansion of foreign engineers into the rest of the United States. In an article titled "Stinking Badges" under the section dealing with "Bootstrap Licensing,"[143] author Steve McConnell writes:

"The movement to license software developers began to gain momentum in 1998 when the Texas Board of Professional Engineers adopted software engineering as a distinct licensable engineering discipline, resulting in a professional engineer, or "P.E.," designation for professional engineers specializing in software.... How many practicing software developers could qualify as professional software engineers under Texas's current licensing procedure? Not very many ... Texas is significant because ... Texas is a bellwether state.... Where Texas goes, others will follow."

Software engineers could not qualify to be professional engineers because they were not trained or tested to be professional engineers, so TBPE simply "waived" them into the country. On February 18, 1998, TBPE stated its intention to recognize software engineering as a legitimate sub-discipline. On June 17, 1998, TBPE approved a license for the Professional Software Engineer, and on August 3, 1998, TBPE began licensing software engineers through a waiver process.[144]

On April 1, 1999, Tobin P. Maginnis, in a discussion of the need for a certification program for Linux software programming technicians, wrote an article in the *Linux Journal* "Linux Certification for the Software Professional" about "a growing discussion concerning the need for certification."[145] Maginnis wrote, "Although certification may not be appropriate for today's Linux enthusiasts, it will be essential in the future as Linux software is brought into corporate and government environments.... Use of the certification process to develop minimal standards that are acceptable to the Linux community will also smooth the coming transition to state board licensure of the Professional Software Engineer." The author acknowledged the "lack of required credentials" and noted "traditional engineers often dismiss computer science as pseudo-engineering."

In order to give engineering globalism a legal foothold in Texas, in 2003 the Texas Legislature passed, and Governor Rick Perry signed into law, an amendment to the Texas Engineering Practice Section 1001.311 "Application by Nonresident" to read:

§ 1001.311. Application by Nonresident

(a) A person who holds a license or certificate of registration issued by another state or a foreign country may apply for a license in this state.

(b) The board may waive any prerequisite to obtaining a license for an applicant after reviewing the applicant's credentials and determining that the applicant holds a license issued by another jurisdiction that has licensing requirements substantially equivalent to those of this state.

No NCEES examinations are required under this rule, and it is impossible for the Texas Board of Professional Engineers to determine "substantial equivalency" with regard to foreign countries or credentials without the examinations having been taken by the applicants. Anyone could receive an engineering license if enough money was pressed into the hands of a Texas board member or state employee. With the adoption of this amendment, the power to grant engineering licensure to foreign nationals was given to a once legitimate, but now corrupted state agency. It is presently unknown how many foreign "pretenders" were allowed into the United States as a result of the Texas Board's actions.

Eventually, on August 11, 2009, the NCEES Board of Directors approved moving forward with the development of a Principles and Practice of Engineering examination, commonly known as the PE exam, for the discipline of software engineering. As reported in the September, 2009 issue of *IEEE-USA Today's Engineer Online*, "As part of the NCEES board action, it was agreed that IEEE-USA will serve as the lead technical society sponsoring the examination with cooperative agreements from other organizations, including the IEEE

Computer Society and the National Society of Professional Engineers.... The jurisdictional licensing boards requesting the examination were those with significant amounts of software engineering industry and those that have institutions granting EAC/ABET-accredited degrees in software engineering. ABET is the accrediting agency for all engineering and technology programs in the United States, and the EAC is responsible for engineering programs in particular."[146]

The IEEE-USA article also noted: "NCEES has an existing 'model law' recommendation that requires: (1) a four-year EAC/ABET-accredited degree in an appropriate engineering discipline, (2) successful completion of an eight-hour fundamentals of engineering examination, (3) verifiable and documented evidence of four years of qualifying engineering experience, and (4) completion of an eight-hour Principles and Practice of Engineering examination. Over the past decade there have been several efforts to establish a path to professional practice licensure for software engineers. These efforts have not been successful due to a variety of issues; however, one of the primary reasons has been the lack of infrastructure to support licensure in accordance with NCEES model law."

On September 20, 2009, an article[147] noted "Partnering with NCEES as co-sponsor of the exam is IEEE-USA, which will be assisted by the IEE Computer Society, the National Society of Professional Engineers and the Texas Board of Professional Engineers.... In Texas, the licensing board for professional engineers began offering licensure to software engineers in 1999 without a standard exam covering software engineering in place. In 2006, the board changed its rules to require all applicants for licensure to pass a PE exam. This change effectively cut off the path to licensure for software engineers in Texas."[148]

Then suddenly, NCEES decided to hold its ground and not create the exam. NCEES might have realized in late 2009 that most potential applicants who would apply to take the exam were not trained sufficiently in their host countries to match the qualifications necessary for licensing professional engineers in the United States. In December 2009, NCEES appears to have reversed itself with regard to creating the exam that would allow foreign nationals to become licensed in the United States, expressing concern about the "cultural differences among different countries."

In the December 2009 NCEES Licensure Exchange newsletter there is the following notation: "The evaluation reports (prepared by the NCEES Credentials Evaluations department) submitted to Member Boards will have some changes. Any deficiencies as they compare to the ABET criteria will be detailed on the front page for quick reference … (Regarding NCEES Criteria Analysis), the decision-makers at Member Boards receiving evaluation reports will be able to see in detail the types of courses an applicant has taken."

The NCEES newsletter continues: "In many cases, deficiencies are in the humanities/social sciences or mathematics/basic sciences categories. It is worthwhile to remember that these types of deficiencies are often the result of differences in education philosophies in different countries. Many countries do not emphasize a liberal arts and sciences curriculum at the college level, concentrating this type of coursework in secondary education."

"For these deficiencies, some boards deny the application and require the candidate to complete additional coursework, while other boards allow the candidate to sit for an exam based on the amount of engineering and design coursework completed."

In effect, the NCEES threw the problem of licensing foreign nationals as software engineers or professional engineers back to the individual states, noting "The ultimate decision rests with the licensing boards." But in Texas, thanks to Governor Rick Perry, the Texas Board of Professional Engineers can no longer be trusted to protect the public.

12

When the time is right, the North American Union, the European Union, the African Union, the Asian Union will all be merged together into a one world government. One bank, one army, one center of power. And if we have learned anything from history. It is that power corrupts, and absolute power corrupts absolutely.

~ North American Union & RFID Chip Truth

In 2002, Governor Rick Perry proposed that Texas enact a massive road and railway plan called the "Trans-Texas Corridor" (TTC). The intention was to have engineers design, and contractors build, thousands of miles of new highways and high-speed trains using public and private money. At the time, Governor Perry kept quiet the fact that the project would accelerate the globalist goal of breaking down the southern border of the United States as a major step toward the establishment of a "North American Union."

Also kept quiet was the fact that a single Spanish corporation called Cintra would be awarded the engineering design and construction contract. Foreign engineers with questionable credentials would design the highway system. The project would cost up to $175 billion over 50 years. The debt would be retired by the motorists who used the roads. Most of the system would be toll roads.

Utilizing the power of eminent domain, the plan for the Trans

Texas Corridor required the state of Texas to acquire nearly 600,000 acres of private property, much of it from Texas farmers and ranchers. Lands taken would also include homes, schools, businesses and churches. Some people who were fearful of losing their property worried that if the appeals that are part of the acquisition procedure failed, then the state of Texas would just simply take the land it wanted. "I wouldn't get too focused on (that)," Assistant Executive Director of the transportation agency Phil Russell said. Referring to what's commonly known as "eminent domain," he said "We've never used it and I don't think we ever will," as noted by The Associated Press.[149]

Governor Rick Perry then hand-picked the members of the Texas Transportation Commission, and the Commission then selected the foreign company to build the highway, leading to questions of cronyism. On December 17, 2004, the *San Antonio Express-News* wrote that the Texas Transportation Commission had "selected a consortium led by Cintra of Spain to build and operate the corridor's first segment of toll roads from Dallas to San Antonio."[150]

In 2005, an arrangement was made between Canada, Mexico and the United States. This arrangement, which was not announced to the public at the time and that Congress is not permitted to regulate, merges the United States, Mexico and Canada into one entity, erasing all borders between the three countries. The arrangement is called the "North American Union."

As evidently envisioned by the Federal Reserve and its international affiliates, (which are considered to be the primary, central source of funding and control of the establishment of the North American Union and the New World Order), a "NAFTA Superhighway" would begin at the southern border of Texas and continue northward, roughly parallel to Interstate 35. Thus it would be of vital importance to the internationalists that a cooperating-governor of Texas—Governor Rick Perry—push forward with the highway agenda. Governor Perry would need engineers to design roads and bridges, ramps, barrier walls, overpasses, and lighting for the NAFTA Superhighway, and the cheaper the engineers were, the greater the profits.

Lou Dobbs reported on CNN:[151]

"The Bush administration's open borders policy and its decision to ignore the enforcement of this country's immigration laws, is part of a broader agenda. President Bush signed a formal agreement that will end the United States as we know it. And he took the step without approval from either the US Congress or the people of the United States."

Lou Dobbs also reported on the banking system uniting the United States, Mexico and Canada with a common currency called the Amero.[152] According to Dobbs:

"The North American Union is a deal that very few people have heard about. It is not a trade agreement. It is a total removal of sovereignty from the United States which will also result in a totally new currency called the Amero—the new currency for the North American community which is being developed right now between Canada, the US and Mexico in order to create a borderless "community" much like the European Union. The intent is to replace the US dollar, the Canadian dollar, and the Mexican peso with the Amero."[153]

The North American Union would consolidate the nations of Mexico, Canada and the United States into a single nation, another step toward the establishment of a New World Order, with the full intention of abolishing the U.S. Constitution. As anticipated, a major transportation system would cut from Mexico, through Texas, then through the heartland of the United States to Canada. New shipping ports would be built at locations along the western edge of Mexico to compete with the western ports in California and drive down labor costs in California. Chinese-made goods would then be shipped through Mexico across the southern border of Texas and into the United States on Governor Rick Perry's NAFTA Superhighway. This

115

arrangement would theoretically help the Mexican government pay the Federal Reserve the massive debt Mexico acquired in the 1970s and 1980s.

As an example of how out-of-control the decades-long "War on Drugs" has become, Governor Rick Perry's Trans-Texas Corridor would also serve as an efficient conduit for the transport of drugs into the United States. Austin, Texas has been an important illegal drug distribution center since the early 1970's. According to a recent article in the Austin American Statesman, ships from China unload methamphetamine precursor chemicals at the port of Lazaro Cardenas north of Acapulco. Much of the population of Luvianos, located near the Mexican port, has migrated into the United States and to Austin in particular. The drugs then enter the United States at Laredo where they are transported northward along Interstate Highway 35 to Austin. Members of a violent Mexican drug gang then use Austin as their base to transport drugs throughout the nation's southern states, the Midwest and also into Illinois, Wisconsin and North Carolina.[154]

On August 18, 2006, *The Dallas Morning News* wrote, "Once again, Gov. Rick Perry's former liaison to the Legislature is working for the Spanish company that won the rights to develop the $7 billion Trans-Texas Corridor. Lobbyist Dan Shelley worked for the firm as a consultant just before he went to the governor's office, a connection first revealed in 2004. State officials denied any connection between that circumstance and the decision three months later, to award Cintra the huge highway contract. Now, Mr. Shelley has left the governor's office, and he and his daughter have large contracts to lobby for the road builder."[155]

An *Associated Press* article dated April 30, 2008 noted: "Gov. Rick Perry appointed former aide Deirdre Delisi of Austin to chair the Texas Transportation Commission ... Delisi, who worked as Perry's chief of staff before stepping down last year, has held assorted jobs in state government and politics, including working as Perry's gubernatorial campaign manager in 2002."[156]

On May 2, 2008, the *San Antonio Express-News* criticized the Delisi pick stating: "But there's also no getting around the fact that the primary reason Perry tapped the 35-year-old Austin resident to head the commission is that she worked for him for nine years as chief of staff, senior deputy chief of staff, deputy chief of staff and director of Perry's 2002 gubernatorial campaign, as well as serving on his staff when he was lieutenant governor and working in his campaign for that office…. The selection of a chairman based on cronyism will further erode public trust."[157]

On January 8, 2009, Carlos Guerra wrote an Op-Ed in the *San Antonio Express-News* stating, "Since drivers already pay federal and state gasoline taxes—supposedly to build and maintain the state's increasingly creaky highway system—the growing army of detractors asked 'Why should they then have to pay to use roads? Isn't that, in fact, double taxation?' " Guerra also noted "Opposition grew even more intense when it became apparent that the tolls would be paid to foreign-owned private contractors—the only investors that stepped forward."[158]

Eventually, the Texas Legislature put a stop to Gov. Perry's plans, or at least slowed them down. However, on May 21, 2010, a Texas watchdog group involved in monitoring Gov. Rick Perry's below-the-radar activities had announced that the governor's Trans-Texas Toll-Road Corridor plan that had once threatened to carve up Texas ranches and farmland as part of the globalist NAFTA superhighway scheme is not as dead as most Texans had assumed. The road building project is now pending in west Texas. Unfortunately, toll roads were given a higher priority in Texas' 2012/13 budget than either public or higher education and the first legs of the highway continue to be under construction.

One problem to the Trans-Texas Highway promoters was that state law requires engineers who design public works systems to be licensed in Texas as professional engineers. Evidently Governor Rick Perry had that problem worked out as well. The effort was made, and continues to be made, to get cheap, foreign technicians into Texas—the ones who have minimal qualifications and no proven regard for public safety—and then have the Texas Board of Professional Engineers title them as "professional engineers."

On August 23, 2006, the Houston Chronicle reported that "More than 14,000 Texans—almost all opposed to the Trans-Texas

Corridor—turned out at Texas Department of Transportation public hearings this summer to express their displeasure with the highway and the governor." About the same time, an "Australian Connection" was being developed to allow international corporations to import foreign engineering technicians into the United States through an Australian organization.

The 1970s movie *The French Connection*[159] featured a theme about the smuggling of drugs from France into New York City. Now in the 2000s there is a real-life "Australian Connection" with a non-stated mission of importing as many fake-engineers as possible from the Middle East and elsewhere into the United States, where they could become licensed as professional engineers in Texas.

In the recent article *PE Report*, the National Society of Professional Engineers noted that the Canadian government is exerting an effort "to make it easier for foreign engineers to become licensed (in Canada because of) 'engineering talent' pouring into the area that can't be used without proper licenses." Canada has minimal education and licensing requirements for licensing these types of "engineers".

The Canadian procedure offers a gateway of opportunity for Islamist extremists who have minimal engineering experience except possibly bomb-making capabilities. They first make their way into Canada where they can become licensed as "PEng" with minimal education and no professional examination, then move to Australia where they await transfer to Texas where they can become fully licensed as "professional engineers."

Not too long ago, Governor Rick Perry was an early endorser of New York politician Rudy Giuliani when Giuliani announced his candidacy for President of the United States. Mr. Giuliani became a partner in the Texas law firm now known as Bracewell Giuliani, the law firm that allegedly advised the Spanish company Cintra as they made toll road investments under Rick Perry's road building agenda. Giuliani reportedly sold off the investment banking arm of his consulting firm to the Macquaire Group, an Australian Group also involved in Gov. Perry's plans to shove toll roads down the throats of Texans.[160]

The Macquarie Group was also reported to have bought up many (if not most) rural Texas newspaper weeklies. The farmers and ranchers of Texas were the property owners who would be most adversely affected by the State of Texas using the power of eminent domain to seize their land; therefore, the need for information control to the large landowners was apparently deemed essential to the Perry group.

By 2008, sensing the mood of the citizenry, the 2008 Texas Republican Platform stated: "We emphatically oppose the Trans-Texas Corridor in any form or manner." Without mentioning any names, the platform stated "We call for full investigation of any public officials authorizing any form of eminent domain for the Trans-Texas Corridor and foreign funding." The platform effort proved to be little more than political theater.

The Texas Board of Professional Engineers quietly deemphasized its attempts to establish software development as a professional engineering discipline. Instead, the Board accelerated its efforts, working toward licensing foreign nationals as multi-disciplined professional engineers whether qualified by education, experience, and examination or not.

During the period of late February thru early March 2008, four members of the Texas engineering board and staff accrued over $17,000 in taxpayer-reimbursed travel, hotels (including the five-star luxury Hotel Realm), and other expenses associated with meeting with representatives of an organization called "Engineers Australia" in Sydney, Australia.[161]

TBPE Board Chairman G. Kemble Bennett, PE, reported in the Summer 2008 edition of *Engineering Express* that "outgoing Board Chairman Mr. Nadkarni, PE" while remaining on the Board, became "assistant vice president for the NCEES Southern Zone, leading the implementation of the NAFTA agreement with Canada and Mexico, evaluating and approving an international agreement with Australia, and working on the Ad Hoc Licensing Committee to finalize some 450 P.E. waiver applications." No evidence has been found that indicates that the 450 foreign nationals to be "waived" and allowed to practice professional engineering in Texas, were capable of meeting either the minimum requirements of the Texas Engineering Practices Act or the NCEES "model law."

The Texas Board of Professional Engineers then adopted a revised rule, making specific reference to Engineers Australia. The rule states "Section 133.27 Application for Temporary License for Engineers Currently Licensed Outside the United States (a) Pursuant to Section 1001.311 of the Act, a temporary license may be issued under this section for applicants who: (1) are citizens of Australia, Canada, or the United Mexican States; (2) are seeking to perform engineering work in Texas for three years or less; (3) are currently licensed or registered in good standing with Engineers Australia or at least one of the jurisdictions of Canada or the United Mexican States; and (4) meet the following experience requirements: (A) Applicant currently registered in Australia shall have at least seven years of creditable engineering experience, three of which must be practicing as a registered engineer with Engineers Australia, as evaluated by the board under Section of this chapter (relating to Experience Evaluation). (B) Applicant currently licensed in Canada or United Mexican States shall: (1) meet the educational requirements of Section 1001.302(a)(1)(A) of the Act and have 12 or more years of creditable engineering experience, as evaluated by the board under Section 133.43 of this chapter; or (ii) meet the educational requirements of Section 1001.302(a)(1)(B) of the Act and have 16 or more years of creditable engineering experience, as evaluated by the board under Section 133.43 of this chapter."

Under the international licensing program for professional engineers currently underway in Texas, the only examination requirement is the ability to pass a test showing that the applicant can speak English. A few months training in an English-speaking telemarketing facility would most likely be considered by TBPE to be sufficient.

The initial effort made by TBPE during the early stages of the Perry administration had been a "foot in the door" attempt to license software developers as "software engineers." That effort was effectively delayed or discontinued with the refusal by the National Council of Engineering Examiners to develop a professional software engineering examination. Now, the Perry-appointed Board has written and implemented Rule Section 133.27, which grants any foreign person with questionable credentials and minimal education, a license to practice professional engineering in Texas without taking and passing the rigid examinations required of American engineers. Rule Section 133.27 affects all engineering disciplines and represents the ultimate "dumbing-down" of any American profession.

Nothing is stated in the Section 133.27 rule that requires the foreign national to pass the NCEES examinations when applying to enter the United States to receive a license as a "professional engineer." Instead, the rule states that the applicant must be "licensed or registered in good standing with Engineers Australia."

So what is Engineers Australia? It is apparently a group, club, cult, tribe, or association of foreign nationals with unknown engineering qualifications. According to a letter dated January 29, 2009, sent from Engineers Australia to the Korea FTA Taskforce, Engineers Australia is an Australian association with 84,000 members involving "engineering practitioners" with a worldwide "membership," and speaks to "licensing requirements ... as (being) significant barriers to trade in professional services," mentioning "passing examinations." The letter is included in the Appendix.

It would appear that Engineers Australia's so called "engineering practitioners" are really engineering technicians or unidentifiable foreign nationals who title themselves as engineers and who are registered with Engineers Australia. The United States maintains its worldwide lead in educating scientists and engineers, and the inferior nature of engineering education in most foreign countries limits the ability of such persons to pass professional examinations.

The letter also states: "While several countries including the United Kingdom, Denmark, Australia, Switzerland and Finland have no, or very limited legal restrictions on the provision of engineering services, the US, Canada, Japan and Singapore operate more restrictive licensing procedures." Mexico is not even mentioned as having proper engineering educational or licensing requirements.

There is even the suggestion of the group claiming the power to restrict individual states in the United States from requiring that the foreign applicants take the major engineering examinations, which are the FE and PE examinations provided by NCEES. Appendix A which is attached to the January 29, 2009 letter, addresses international agreements and undergraduate education, noting "the purpose of the agreement is that engineers entered on the APEC Engineer Register will be granted a high degree of mutual exemption from further assessment when practicing in … the United States."

On the last page is written: "The APEC Engineer Register can also work as a framework for the development of bilateral mutual recognition agreements. This process has developed out of frustration that engineers entered on the APEC Engineer Register have not yet been granted a high degree of mutual exemption from further assessment when practising (sic) in any of the participating economies."

Thus, foreign nationals are "frustrated" that they have not been able to meet the normal qualification requirements expected for the practice of professional engineering in the United States. As a substitute for qualifications, according to Engineers Australia and apparently as agreed to by the Texas Board of Professional Engineers, no professional examinations are required to practice engineering in Texas if the foreign national is registered with Engineers Australia. There is a vast difference between being "registered" on a list, and being "licensed" to practice a profession in the United States. And once in the country, the 84,000 so called-engineers can easily branch out to every state in the United States. That's enough men for a small army.

As noted previously, it is well known in international engineering circles that paying a bribe for engineering credentials in foreign countries is commonplace. The January 29, 2009, letter written by an Engineers Australia official was sent to an official in South Korea. For those people who have long memories, Watergate lawyer John McCloy reported extensively on the bribes demanded by government officials of South Korea, and also Saudi Arabia, during the investigation of Gulf Oil payoffs in the 1970s.

Almost since the beginning of Rick Perry's governorship, he has placed an emphasis on "tort reform" or what he calls "too much suing." Tort reform in Texas has enabled corporate homebuilders and insurance companies to minimize losses from lawsuits and claims brought by aggrieved consumers. Tort reform has also maximized profits for insurance companies that have also increased premiums.

Binding arbitration now denies citizen access to the courts in Texas. Aggrieved Texans who unknowingly buy deficient houses or who are investors swindled by Ponzi schemes, usually find in the fine print of their contracts that they had committed themselves to engage in binding arbitration and that they had foregone their constitutional rights to trial by jury.

Rick Perry was sworn into office as Texas governor in January 2001 and the first evidence of potential bribery found within the Texas engineering board records, occurred in early 2002. That incident did not involve a foreign citizen at all. It involved an American citizen who, once he became licensed as a professional engineer, would serve to benefit two groups of Rick Perry's largest contributors—representatives of general business corporations and large corporate homebuilders. Eventually, the engineer would wind up testifying at arbitration hearings as a professional engineer against many new homebuyers who had been tricked into buying shoddily-constructed homes. Those buyers had then been forced into dealing with their builder by trying to work with a new Perry-backed state agency—the Texas Residential Construction Commission—and then subsequently the buyers would face binding arbitration where the rules of legal procedure are almost non-existent and an engineer-perjurer would not be closely scrutinized.

The engineer's job was to convince arbitrators that he was an engineering expert in home construction matters and that there was little-to-nothing wrong with the home. Often an arbitrator is a lawyer whose income depends on repeat business from large corporations—including homebuilders—and the engineer's job was to testify in a manner that would artificially lower or totally negate the amount of money the builder would have to pay the homebuyer to repair their home. Based on the engineer's testimony, the arbitrator would then award, for example, $7,000 to the homebuyer for a house that would cost over $150,000 to repair.

Thus, the engineer and arbitrators together would financially benefit the large corporate, Wall-Street financed insurance corporations, and also benefit the large corporate homebuilders that were so deeply involved in the mortgage fraud that has now engulfed most of the financial world. It is no wonder that homebuilders contributed so much money to Gov. Rick Perry—their senior executives and major stockholders made out like bandits by not having to pay hardly anything out on consumer claims.

Texas is not Mexico or South Korea. Before the days of Rick Perry, it was not very easy to walk into the office of a state agency and offer a high ranking public official a lot of money to make sure a certain person is allowed to become licensed as a professional engineer. It takes pressure from above, and in Texas, that pressure can come from the governor's office.

The engineer "person of interest" had attended the University of Texas at Austin, making "C"s and "D"s in many of his engineering subjects. The college transcript that the Texas engineering board relied on to grant him a license to practice engineering shows that he spent time in his college years on scholastic probation and does not show that he ever graduated.

The record indicates that about the time he left UT he was working at a public swimming pool facility for the City of Austin. He also worked as a draftsman, not as an engineer trainee. No signed reference forms have been found in his records. He was then arrested for driving a vehicle while under the influence of alcohol and/or drugs. He was found guilty and later violated his probation.

He applied to take the NCEES examinations that are required to gain a license to practice but failed to pass the exam. He applied again, and failed again. Upon his request to have his second exam rescored, NCEES refused. It was at this point that pressure was believed to have been applied against state employees in order that the person of interest could become licensed as a professional engineer.

A front-side copy of a check dated early 2002, payable to the Texas Board of Professional Engineers, has appeared in the public record. At the base of the check is written "Rescore exam". The check was drawn on a bank where banking officials were recently unable to determine if it was a check at all since the item bore no bank routing numbers at the bottom of the check. The check also bore the name of an engineering firm that had gone out of business in 1995.

It is believed that the copy of the check found in the files of the Texas Board of Professional Engineers is a fake, placed in the applicant's record in case someone in the future might question if the Board had rescored the exam for free or had charged a fee.

Regardless, state employees with the agency then changed the applicant's NCEES-administered engineering test score (in pencil) and granted a license for him to practice professional engineering in Texas. Soon after that, some of the people directly involved in the matter left state employment, with at least one of the former state-employees being deeded a million dollars worth of real estate.

One recent rule addition to the Engineering Practices Act specifically requires Texas professional engineers to comply with international law while at the same time, as American citizens, they are supposed to comply with U.S Constitutional law: "Section 131.15(a) (3) Compliance and Enforcement Committee. The committee shall meet as required to evaluate issues and possibly develop proposed actions for the full board on enforcement issues. The committee may participate in activities such as evaluating rules concerning enforcement of the Act; reviewing the progress of major enforcement cases or groups of cases; suggesting sanctions for violations of the Act; participation in national and international engineering law enforcement activities on the board's behalf; providing general guidance to the executive director on enforcement issues; and evaluating any other issue indirectly or directly relating to engineering law enforcement."

Rule Section 133.27 along with Section 131.15(a)(3), allows the State of Texas to violate the constitutional rights of American engineers while showing preference to corporate business interests foreign to the United States.

The Texas Board of Professional Engineers has indeed "gone corrupt" on behalf of Governor Rick Perry and his globalist cohorts. However, it is not yet too late to put a stop to their nefarious deeds. This kind of corruption can be exposed for what it is.

As to the overall effect of the actions of Governor Rick Perry's

Texas Board of Professional Engineers on the continued practice of engineering by American engineers, the prospects are not good and inevitably national security will be jeopardized. It can be expected that the new NAFTA system of trying to license foreign nationals in Texas will be extended to many states in the United States if the attempt in Texas is not blocked by what has been a Perry-friendly Texas legislature, Congress, or the courts.

13

☙ IMPEACHABLE MOMENTS – THREE
DAYS IN MARCH ❧

These capitalists generally act harmoniously and in concert to
fleece the people, and now that they have got into a quarrel
with themselves, we are called upon to appropriate the people's
money to settle the quarrel.

~ Abraham Lincoln's speech to the Illinois
legislature, January, 1837

The nation's two political parties, both the Democratic Party and
the Republican Party, no long represent the interests of the
individual American citizens, most of whom only want to live their
lives in freedom, peace, and with limited government regulation; not
within the sphere of a centralized, one world government with a
globalist-controlled one-world economy and an American military
dominating and rebuilding foreign nations at the loss of American
treasure and blood. For decades, Americans divided in every way
possible have gone to the polls to vote for one of the two "least
offensive" political candidates who are actually pre-selected during the
party primary process.

The video *North American Union & RFID Chip Truth* states: "A
centralized, one world economy depends on totalitarian elements of
chaos and separation based on religion, patriotism, race, wealth, class,
and every other form of arbitrary and separatist identification to create
a controlled population malleable in the hands of the few. 'Divide and
Conquer' is the motto. As long as people continue to see themselves as
separate from everyone else, they lend themselves to becoming

completely enslaved. The 'men behind the curtain' know this and they also know that if people ever realized the truth of their relationship to nature and the truth of their personal power, the entire manufactured Zeitgeist they prey upon would collapse like a house of cards."[162]

Throughout 2007, leading into the campaign for the Democratic nomination for President of the United States, Senator Hillary Clinton maintained a lead over Senator Obama. National polls taken during the autumn of 2007 showed Clinton ahead of Obama by wide margins. By the end of 2007, Clinton appeared to be almost assured of gaining the Democratic presidential nomination.

The Iowa Democratic caucus took place on January 3, 2008, and Obama won with 37.6 percent of the vote to Clinton's 29.4 percent. Soon thereafter, on January 31, 2008, the *Wall Street Journal* announced that former Federal Reserve Chairman Paul Volcker would become one of Obama's backers.[163]

With Volcker's endorsement of Obama, campaign cash flowed directly and indirectly to the DNC and Mr. Obama, and Senator Clinton found herself losing numerous state primaries until by late February 2008, Clinton was in a "must win" situation headed into Texas and Ohio. In Texas, Clinton defeated Obama by 51% to 47.4 % in the Democratic popular vote but lost the delegate count in a complicated and questionable caucus process. After that, Obama defeated Clinton in the other party primaries and the caucuses, winning the endorsement of the 2008 Democratic National Convention to compete with Republican Senator John McCain for the presidency.

The early months of 2008 were filled with controversy within the Democratic Party ranks. By using the caucus and "super-delegate" system, the Democratic National Committee had been able to ignore the democratic primary voters who had voted for Hillary Clinton as the nomination process descended into chaos at the caucuses. Many Democrats who had voted for Senator Clinton contended that their votes did not elect the nominee, and that instead the DNC had "selected" Obama for the nomination in a manner reminiscent of voter fraud often observed in third-world nations.

Ms. Gigi Gaston, granddaughter of a Democratic governor of

Massachusetts, produced a video titled *We Will Not Be Silenced*.[164] The video features several witnesses who testified how the 2008 Democratic primary caucuses were filled with violations of party rules and were fraught with malicious practices unacceptable in any election in any free republic—practices that violated the core democratic principle of one person, one vote. By the Democratic National Committee gaming the system in such a manner, the illegal activities produced a huge impact.

Democrats filed complaints over the caucus process in many states. There were at least 2,000 complaints filed in Texas alone. The Obama "change" campaign had created and encouraged armies of amoral individuals across the nation who had stormed the caucuses, stolen caucus packets, falsified documents, changed the results, allowed children and unregistered people to vote, scared and intimidated Clinton supporters, stalked them, threatened them with death or injury, intimidated Latinos and African-Americans who wanted to vote for Clinton, locked Clinton supporters out of their polling places, silenced their voices by shouting them down or threatening them, and otherwise engaged in multiple instances of fraud. The illegal activities undertaken in Obama's name ultimately impacted the United States, a country that eventually elected the man to be President although there is no assurance that the process reflected the true intent of the American people; including the fact that Diebold voting machines were used in several states. Diebold machines have been shown to be easy to hack, and give fraudulent voting results.[165]

As one of the Clinton workers explained in *We Will Not Be Silenced,* in referring to the Obama supporters: "They knew how to corrupt the process." Another worker said the Obama supporters "inundated the process. The strategy was to overwhelm the system and in the chaos that ensued they could steal the election." Rather than investigate and penalize this otherwise illegal activity, "the Democratic Party rewarded it by allowing it to stand" according to the video.

The Federal Reserve most likely believed that a President Obama could be manipulated to give the national and international financial elites what they wanted, since by the end of 2008 the economy could no longer sustain the many previous years of insider trading and other forms of corruption on Wall Street. Through Paul Volcker, the Fed appears to have given Obama its support. It just took money plus a timed financial manipulation of the economy and Wall Street a few weeks before the election to collapse the financial markets, panic enough voters to push Obama over the top, and elect him to the presidency instead of Republican Senator John McCain. Almost immediately after the election, President Obama was pushing to give the Federal Reserve and FDIC more power and control.

On September 15, 2008, the investment-banking firm Lehman Brothers filed for bankruptcy after the Federal Reserve and US Treasury Department refused to bail out the company. Then came a financial panic that resulted in an excessively expensive US government bailout of favored financial corporations in both the U.S and Europe.

The Federal Reserve had been engaging in insider trading for years. The Fed-favored American investment companies and banks are still unknown to the American citizen, and will remain unknown until the Federal Reserve is totally audited; however, two of those favored firms are suspected to be: Merrill Lynch, which the Fed forcibly merged into Bank of America; and American International Group, known as AIG.

AIG's main business is insurance. AIG was also one of the corporations that sold hundreds of billions of dollars worth of credit-default swap mortgage derivatives to anyone who would buy them. As the markets began to panic, AIG's national and international financial elitists suddenly found themselves in financial trouble. An AIG bankruptcy would have cut off their foreign bank investments and bonuses, and unlike their predecessors' reactions during the Great Depression of the 1930s, these modern-day robber barons were not about to jump out of office-building windows. They wanted their money fast in the form of bank bailouts and monetary bonuses, and only the U.S. taxpayers could give that money to them.

On October 21, 2008, right before the presidential and congressional elections, the *Wall Street Journal* reported: "When the (Obama) team discusses the financial crisis, 'the most important question to Obama: What does Paul Volcker think?'... Senator Obama said, 'Let me tell you who I associate with. On economic policy, I associate with Warren Buffett and former Fed Chairman Paul Volcker ... who have shaped my ideas and who will be surrounding me in the White House.' "[166]

For three days in March 2009, the Federal Reserve manipulated the newly inaugurated President Obama into committing what could be considered an impeachable offense—illegally transferring U.S. taxpayer assets to foreign banks and therefore violating Article I, Section 9 of the United States Constitution: "No money shall be drawn from the Treasury but in consequence of appropriations made by law." In the process, the international elites who had gamed the U.S. economy were paid off by the U.S. taxpayers. President Barack Obama had become just another Federal Reserve puppet.

According to media reports, on March 16, 2009, Rep. Barney Frank, chairman of the House Financial Services Committee, "noted that the Federal Reserve Board ... was the institution that gave AIG its initial government bailout, before Congress passed legislation providing for additional assistance, and said that not enough safeguards were built into the deal. It was also revealed that AIG used more than $90 billion in federal aid to pay foreign and domestic banks, some of which had received their own multibillion-dollar U.S. government bailouts. Some of the biggest recipients of the AIG money were Goldman Sachs at $12.9 billion, and three European banks—France's Societe Generale at $11.9 billion, Germany's Deutsche Bank at $11.8 billion and Britain's Barclays PLC at $8.5 billion. Merrill Lynch, which also was undergoing federal scrutiny of its bonus plans, received $6.8 billion as of December 31, 2008."[167]

On March 17, 2009, it was reported that "While the Senate was constructing the $787 billion stimulus (during the month before, Senate Banking Committee Chairman Christopher) Dodd added an executive-compensation restriction to the bill." The provision, now called "The Dodd Amendment" by the Obama Administration, provides an "exception for contractually obligated bonuses agreed to before Feb. 11, 2009—which exempts the very AIG bonuses Dodd and the others are now seeking to tax." Dodd's original amendment did not include that exemption, and the Connecticut Senator denied inserting the provision. "I can't point a finger at someone who was responsible for putting those dates in," Dodd told FOX. "I can tell you this much, when my language left the Senate, it did not include it. When it came back, it did…. Because of negotiations with the Treasury Department and the bill conferees, several modifications were made," Dodd Spokesperson Kate Szostak said. Separately, Senator Dodd was AIG's largest single recipient of campaign donations during the 2008 election cycle with $103,100… also one of AIG Financial Products' largest offices is based in Connecticut.[168] Dodd later stated that the Obama administration had asked him to insert a provision that had the effect of authorizing AIG's bonuses.[169]

On March 18, 2009, "Senator Ron Wyden, D-Ore, all but pointed the finger of blame directly at the 'Obama economic team' (headed by Volcker) for allegedly stripping a provision from the stimulus package last month that would have slapped a heavy tax on bonuses like the ones doled out at AIG." Wyden and Senator Olympia Snowe, R-Maine, had included a provision to tax executive bonuses that was later stripped.[170] Both Wyden and Snowe "battled administration officials" but Wyden said, "I was never able to convince them that this was something that ought to be included."

The Wyden-Snowe provision was mysteriously dropped in the early February closed-door negotiations over the stimulus bill—intense meetings that involved Treasury Secretary Timothy Geithner, Obama economic adviser Larry Summers, White House Chief of Staff Rahm Emanuel, and budget director Peter Orszag, as well as senior Democrat members of Congress.[171] The afternoon of March 18, 2009, Fox News Network identified those "senior Democrat members of Congress" as Speaker of the House Nancy Pelosi and Senate Majority Leader Harry Reid.

Without Wyden's and Snowe's Senate vote that had included the provision, the stimulus package would not have passed the U.S. Senate; the foreign banks and individuals would not have been paid off through congressional appropriation; and furthermore, the Federal Reserve would have had to recall and replenish the US Treasury with the bailout money it had already paid to the foreign banks. It appears obvious that both U.S. Senators Wyden and Snowe, plus possibly Senator Dodd, were deceived by the Federal Reserve and the Obama administration in a manner that would benefit foreign banks with tremendous adverse consequences to U.S. taxpayers, and there was no meeting of the minds regarding the passage of the stimulus package before President Obama signed it into law. The executive bonus issue is the "smoke"; the "fire" is the transfer of taxpayer dollars to foreign entities.

American taxpayers are not only supporting AIG executives and AIG itself, but are also being used to prop up foreign institutions and individuals in apparent violation of the U.S. Constitution, in what is most likely the greatest theft of taxpayer money in the history of the United States.

14

ॐ **CONVENTION NOTES** ॐ

*Freedom is never more than one generation away from
extinction. We didn't pass it to our children in the
bloodstream. It must be fought for, protected, and handed on
for them to do the same.*

~ Ronald Reagan

The only way for America to begin the task of getting back to a
Constitutional form of government with a real (not fake) market
economy, is for presidential candidate Ron Paul to acquire at least 50
percent of the Republican delegates *before* the August, 2012 Republican
National Convention. No other presidential candidate, including
incumbent Obama, is willing or able to take on such a task.

During a recent Internet "blogfest" between a Rick Perry
supporter and a Ron Paul supporter, the Perry supporter wrote: "Well
you will have your choice. You can be a purest all you want but in the
end you will have to vote for whichever Republican name is on the
ballot, or vote for Obama."

The Perry supporter is absolutely correct. The only time
Americans do have a real choice of who is going to lead the nation as
President of the United States, is during the Republican and
Democratic primaries in each state. That is the only time that citizens
have an opportunity to get the best candidates on the ballot.

Americans also need a heightened sense of what happens to their
vote after the primaries are over. Americans need to actively
participate in the primary process to assure themselves and the nation
that their votes really are counted and not stolen.

The video *We Will Not Be Silenced*[172] provides an excellent accounting of how elements of the DNC political machine were able to break rules and steal the Democratic nomination from Senator Hillary Clinton and award the nomination to Barack Obama during the spring primary caucuses of 2008. No similar video has yet emerged of how the RNC Republican Party machine also broke rules and stole delegates from Representative Ron Paul to benefit Senator John McCain at the same time; however, I was present at a Senatorial District GOP Convention that took place in Travis County, Texas and I did take notes.

Both political parties depend on acquiring vast sums of money donated by large organizations for political campaigns. The Republican National Committee is the only group allowed by law to provide direct financial support to the GOP presidential candidate, and also the Democratic National Committee is the only group allowed to provide direct financial support to the Democratic presidential candidate. Most of the people who become delegates or who work at the conventions, are people who volunteer their time and try to participate in a fair elective process for the voters; however, at the upper level of machine politics, there is no way to know for sure if money is exchanged among a small number of people at the highest levels to make sure that one or two people are able to break certain rules at critical times in the process.

As a result of the political manipulations that take place at the state conventions, once the primaries, the state conventions, and the national conventions are over, the typical American voter is faced with the choice of voting for the "lesser of two evils" in the general election. Many people are not buying into that concept any longer and a lot of well-informed citizens are waking up to the truth as time goes on and participating in the primary process. Many will agree that individual rights and freedoms have been usurped by the misdeeds within the political machinery of both the Democratic and Republican parties—those political machines that include state legislators and governors who are at the apex of control of the convention process.

There is minimal public accounting of the amount of money that is passed through banks, large corporations, and American straw-man lawyers—those who receive money from foreign corporations and governments—to politicians running for office. An honest seeker of office has a hard time getting enough money to continue. The dishonest seeker of office will sell his soul to get what he and his wealthy enablers want. Most of those politicians, especially the incumbents who have made their entire life's work a practice of soaking money from the public, will lie to the American people to hold onto power and do exactly what the corporations want. A recent tabulation of members of both houses of Congress indicates that there are 51 members who have served 30 plus years; 38 members with 40 plus years; and 6 members who have served 50 plus years. Term limits are certainly in order.

The end goal for the enablers is to continue to divide and conquer we American individuals, take away our identity as human beings, and make sure that very few of us acquire and retain enough wealth to compete with them. Those people who struggle just to get by are no threat to the enablers. Those people with an entrepreneurial spirit, who rise high enough above the heap to become a competitive force, will often get targeted and, unless they are very lucky, will get knocked down. Businesspeople have to use commercial banks, and everything they do financially is on a computer accessible to the officers and directors of the New York banks, the OCC, the FDIC and the Federal Reserve. And when businesses are audited by the state government, everything must be disclosed as well, with no assurance that the information will not be provided to competitors, as has recently occurred in Texas.

The mission of the Federal bankers is to make the Americans either dependent on government or to work like slaves. The mission is also to deceive us and to take away most of our money, our property, and our freedoms, but leave us with just enough to buy cheap products that are made in other countries. It is doubtful that many of the existing elected officials in both parties who benefit from the financial largesse of corporations and government agencies want to change any of this. So what can the American people do about it?

The answer is that the American people need to get seriously involved in the primary and precinct process and make sure that they know everything about the background of a candidate for office. Children who play organized baseball are required to show a birth certificate. Why shouldn't a political candidate to high office be required to do the same?

In the spring of 2008, I was elected along with others to represent my voting precinct as a convention delegate to the Senatorial GOP Convention held in Travis County on March 29, 2008. At the convention I was enthralled by the young people trying to be heard, and very disappointed by the party apparatus that I saw break the rules in every way possible to shut the young people out. I saw that the game was fixed against the young people even at this lower level of politics.

But I was also very enthused by the effort of the young people who refused to take "no" for an answer, which gave me hope that at a future convention the young people, who have already been sacrificed to the debts of their elders, will find a way to overcome the political machinery that confronts them.

The precinct level is where American citizens can again regain control of the destiny of our country. Here are my notes taken that day:

I am a precinct delegate in Precinct 359 at the Senate District 14 convention but today I passed up an opportunity to go further to the State convention in order to enable a younger delegate from my precinct to participate (we were allocated only one delegate). I am 65 years old, a believer in our Constitution and our individual liberties, and first voted for Barry Goldwater against Lyndon Johnson here in liberal Democrat Travis County and have continuously voted as a conservative Republican ever since. I attended the SD14 convention today (first time) because I wanted to know what occurred before a national convention.

The national conventions (Democrats too) have become Hollywood-staged for prime time TV. Problem has been that they have become so boring that many people have stopped watching, which is the desired result of those in power who are trying to keep the American people asleep. The conventions of the 1950s and 1960s, on radio and then TV, used to have inspiring speeches, open debate, Chet Huntley and David Brinkley and Walter Cronkite, even fisticuffs between delegates with the sergeant-at-arms hauling them out (no tasers back then), and people yelling and screaming their positions and really behaving in a disgracefully democratic and non-politically correct way. That was what American politics was really about. Not this polite ho-hum flowers, good-hair and perfume canned-stuff both parties have stuffed into our faces for so many years.

I arrived at Delco Center at 8 am; stood in line about 30 minutes to register. A young man was handing out yellow fliers to everyone in line, titled "Vote FOR the Minority Report of Robert Morrow." He wore Ron Paul buttons on his shirt. Out of 16 delegates and alternates elected at the recent precinct 359 convention, 9 of us had been willing to spend this Saturday engaging in the democratic process. (Two additional people who had previously been at our precinct convention were apparently Demo infiltrators and they did not show up for today's convention). Roll call indicated limited attendance from most large precincts, although the small precincts had most or all of their delegates show up.

Committees had met the previous week. Those committees evidently consisted of "old party" plus some new entrants into Republican Party. Resolutions Committee had issued report encompassing 2006 platform; but apparently all of the amendments proposed at our own precinct convention had been given "short shrift."

Convention started about 9:30 am. Then there was an estimated thirty-nine percent spattering of polite applause for aggie Governor Rick Perry with a few "moos" or "boos."

Next 5 hours were spent debating and voting on the single Rules Committee Minority Report of Robert Morrow and other matters. Vote of our precinct was 4 yes (in favor of the Minority Report), 3 no and 2 abstentions. Actual vote out of around 1600 attendees was about 49% for and 51% against.

Evidently, the Ron Paul turnout in the small precincts had been high, and old guard was worried about it so committee had voted to exclude 95 small precincts because they were afraid of the Ron Paul support. After the adverse vote results were announced, when a young woman (and committee volunteer) proposed from the floor that, because of the close vote, an equitable adjustment be made so that the Morrow minority report could be reflected in the minority precinct totals, the chairman told her to put it in writing. Business proceeded for a few minutes, and when the young woman returned to the microphone and submitted it in writing she was ruled out of order and out of luck.

Some Ron Paul supporters walked out at this point. Personally, I was disappointed at what I had just witnessed. Before the count had been totaled—and also thereafter—speakers at the podium reflected on what was happening to the Republican Party and why the party is in trouble, and I sat there with about 1,600 other people and saw it for myself. Exclusion of points of view and lack of transparency must not be tolerated at any level. First, the committee obviously stacked their report to exclude the wishes of 95 precincts. Next, 49 percent of the attendees were in favor of the minority report, but the way it shook out, the wishes of those 49 percent were excluded. That left us with about 800 delegates angry; and 800 delegates semi happy but even they were not happy because when I caucused with them in my own precinct I learned that the big things to all of us including the minority was (1) close the borders, (2) no amnesty, (3) no more illegal immigration with hospitals and schools suffering from it, (4) no NAFTA—get the mega corporations with their 35,000 K-street lawyer-lobbyists out of their corrupt partnerships with the federal government, all of whom work against the American small businessman and woman, (5) right to life, (6) our Middle East policy and (7) shut down the Federal Reserve. NO ONE in my precinct caucus, nor people in other precincts I spoke to, was in favor of our government or our party being dominated by the big New York bank /House of Morgan "Rockefeller Republicans" selling out this country through the Federal Reserve to Saudis or China or France or the Queen or anyone else with their CFR and their NAFTA and NWO.

I spoke with a woman who had previously been a delegate to the State Republican Convention. She told me that it was just as fixed there as what we had just witnessed, and good luck even getting passed any amendments to the platform not already sanctioned by the "old guard". Nevertheless, she said that it is important to get viewpoints to the State convention and even national convention and speak to the committees because some of them might think the same way you do.

Now, I've worked on a lot of political campaigns in my life. What I have to say to the Republican Party is that they had better start listening to the young people wanting to enter the party and who are being rebuffed by the old party "Legacy". It's their future at risk. Obama is attracting a lot of young people on his own, and both parties are in trouble with all the corruption. What I witnessed today was EXCLUSION of points of view so that the Republicans can have a "sanitized convention" (and extremely boring one) for Senator John McCain. I doubt that I will waste the electricity to my TV to turn the convention on, and I believe I am in the majority on that one unless something happens.

My notes stopped at that point. As the convention was winding down, I saw long lines of people, mostly young primary delegates, waiting to be interviewed by the GOP old guard so that they might be sent to the State Convention through the open delegate process. Talking with a few of them, it was obvious to me that because they were young they intended to vote for Ron Paul. As I left the convention hall, I became very depressed and angry because I realized that few, if any of them, would be selected as open delegates. Obviously the Republican Party machine was just as dishonest as I had heard the Democratic Party machine had become.

If I am ever elected to be a precinct delegate again, I intend to take a video camera, "wear a wire", or do whatever it takes to record the kind of dishonesty I witness during the convention if it should occur again; and then I will get with others and file a civil lawsuit against the Republican party, or a criminal complaint with the district attorney, for taking our money but then fraudulently manipulating the rules and stealing the election. Convention attendees all over the nation should consider doing the same, no matter which political party they participate in. The right to vote in our country is a sacred thing and we don't need dishonest people at the higher level of the political process stealing our votes and stealing our nation.

Constant vigilance at all the conventions around the country will be more important than ever in 2012. For any number of reasons, the GOP has changed its winner-take-all rules for the 2012 elections and at last word, any state that holds a primary or caucus before April 1, 2012 must not award its delegates on a winner-take-all basis, and instead must award its delegates on a proportional basis. This means that if a front-runner, say "true-Constitutional conservative" Ron Paul, whom the GOP establishment appears to greatly fear, receives a 40 percent plurality in a five-way split field, as the front-runner he would get only 40 percent of the delegates instead of at least 50-plus percent needed to have a majority of delegates. This will keep second-tier candidates in the race and could deny the front runner (Paul) the immediate nomination.

A deal could be made at that point. If the front-runner wanted the nomination for President, he or she could be forced to consider a more New World Order type of individual for the vice-presidency, such as what happened to Ronald Reagan when he had to choose New

World Order advocate George H.W. Bush as his running mate. The nominees to both positions can be chosen by the party establishment in such a manner, unless the front-runner has at least 50 percent of the delegates already committed before the first balloting begins at the national convention.

Assuming Rick Perry drops out of the running before the conclusion of the primary season, and if no candidate holds a majority of the delegates at the time of first balloting, then non-primary candidates could then be nominated after the first inclusive ballot. That nomination could include anyone who had not run in the primaries or who had dropped out during primary season—including Chris Christi and Rick Perry. Using a story line similar to the 1960s film version of *The Manchurian Candidate*, former House Speaker Newt Gingrich, a gifted orator, could bring the convention delegates and the nation to its feet, rousing all viewers to "take the White House by storm" and "throw out that rascal Obama." And then who should walk into the spotlight from behind the curtain, up to the podium and deliver a powerful speech that had been four years in its development and that had been rehearsed for over a year? None other than tall, suave, handsome, good-hair-actor, Texas Governor Rick Perry himself.

And when Perry finishes his speech, his earlier blunders would be forgotten. The roaring crowd would stand at attention as a 200-piece band marches through the arena playing *The Battle Hymn of the Republic*, while balloons fall from the ceilings and television viewers across the land shout, "Yes! He Is The One!" To a person who thinks Rick Perry is a real conservative, the mere thought of the scene brings tears to the eyes and makes one want to put down this book, rise to one's feet and salute!

The nation would then be forced to choose between Rick Perry and incumbent President Barack Obama. Which one would you, the reader, choose?

Polls indicate a majority of U.S. military personnel support Ron Paul's candidacy for President. Tens of thousands of military servicemen and women are stationed far away from this country and have to vote absentee. The fraud that sometimes takes place in the delayed or non-counting of absentee-military votes must not be allowed to happen again in 2012.

Polls also indicate a sizeable number of Democrats also support Ron Paul's candidacy. In many states there are deadlines for Democrats to temporarily change parties in order to vote in the Republican primaries.

It is going to take the states sending at least 50 percent of pledged Ron Paul delegates to the Republican national convention, for Ron Paul to win on the first ballot. Only after then can Ron Paul really begin the initial steps that are needed to defeat President Obama, defeat the Federal Reserve and the New World Order; and help save the country for future generations of Americans.

But the new president will also need a Congress willing to do the right thing to help the new president. Every congressional prospect needs to pledge his or her loyalty to the Constitution; because that's the only real weapon against tyranny that we, the people of the United States, still barely have left.

15

∂ʰ AN AMERICAN SPRING ∞

*If you want to make an omelet, you must be willing to break
a few eggs.*

~ Robespierre, architect of the reign of
terror, Revolutionary France

The ultimate question is, will the presidential candidate who people
are seriously considering voting for, fall under the dictates of
secret groups: the Federal Reserve, the Bilderberg Group, the CFR, the
New World Order, the large international corporations, or any other
group that is working against the constitutional rights of individual
American citizens—will that candidate do what those groups want? In
the matter of Governor Rick Perry, it is highly likely that the answer
would be "yes, most assuredly." Nomination of such a person to the
highest office in the land will inevitably lead to serious trouble for the
nation in the same manner that his tenure as governor has led to
serious trouble for Texas.

As for Mr. Gingrich, Mr. Romney and Mr. Cain, they can be
expected to remain loyal to the dictates of the Federal Reserve and
Wall Street, and the other secret groups as well; as has the current
president, Barack Obama, remained loyal to their dictates. But if the
Federal Reserve's candidate wins this next election, it is doubtful that
the nation will be willing to take much more. In an Austin American
Statesman opinion article titled "Talking about a Revolution over the
U.S. Economy," writer Scott Burns questioned if the "scent of tear gas
is in our future," and after quoting Robespierre, Mr. Burns wrote "The
coming American Spring is going to be tough. Many eggs need to be

broken if we are to save our country. It will start to happen when we begin to tell the politicians they have done enough for us. That we want no more."[173]

Mr. Burns also noted, "Republicans fake it when they argue to cut taxes because the cuts 'pay for themselves' through higher federal revenues. Democrats fake it when they spend more but call it 'investment.' The witless conspiracy of our two parties has brought the country to bankruptcy. It has to end. Not over 10 years. Not in (or on) another generation. It has to end now, with sacrifice for all. If it means voting every single existing politician out of office, so be it. If my reader mail is any indication, we could have a national recall and start over right now."

Mr. Burns then listed some of the eggs that will need to go into the new American omelet. I have included below some of Mr. Burns' suggestions as well as some of my own:

1. Break the back of the finance/banking complex that continues to play heads-they-win, tails-you-lose ball. The change from George W. Bush to Barack Obama proved there is only one party in America—the Institutional Party, the party of finance, also known as the Federal Reserve. We can change this by adopting limited-purpose banking. This is banking where the bankers aren't making their profits and bonuses with our money while having their extravagant risk back-stopped by our taxes.

2. Whip the insurance/medical complex of vested interests that pushed President George W. Bush to create a guaranteed income for the pharmaceutical and insurance industries with Medicare Part D, and also pushed President Barack Obama to do basically the same thing with Obamacare. Let the pharmaceutical companies produce products at competitive, non-semi-monopolistic prices that people can afford, and require all insurance companies to offer a smorgasbord of

insurance products that allow people to pick and choose what they want; and compete with each other in every state.

3. Get real about unlimited health care entitlement. It has been estimated that 10 to 30 percent of Medicare spending is lost to fraud and another 30 percent of all medical care is unnecessary.

4. Cut defense spending wisely and change foreign policy. Keep a sharp eye on Iran but build a more mobile defense capability and spend only as much as the next five largest military spenders rather than the next 20 nations.

5. Phase out all NAFTA trade policies and put a stop to the Federal Reserve's efforts to create a North American Union. This nation needs to get back to a realistic balanced trade policy by permanently extinguishing former President George H. W. Bush's "thousand points of light," which along with the people behind the Federal Reserve have become the basis of the demonic "New World Order."

6. Take apart the hated "Patriot Act" to eliminate unconstitutional provisions and force the government to adhere to rights of due process. If Congress refuses to change the Patriot Act, then keep replacing Congress until a new Congress changes it.

Add to this list a complete restructuring of our tax structure. Restructure our regulatory structure including gutting the job-costing Environmental Protection Agency, the overreaching FDIC and numerous other federal agencies.

With regard to globalism and constitutional rights, the two are not mutually compatible. As noted by University of San Diego law

Professor David S. Law:[174]

"The challenge of making commitments that others will find persuasive is particularly acute for governments. Ordinary actors can make their commitments credible by rendering them in the form of legally binding agreements subject to government enforcement. By contrast, when the government itself breaks its word, third-party enforcement is generally unavailable. It is thus difficult, if not impossible, for a sovereign to make a commitment that is truly inviolable. Some sovereign commitments, however, are more credible than others. The extent that a constitutional commitment to the rights of investors or workers is especially difficult for the state to undo or ignore, the credibility of that commitment is enhanced accordingly.

"If a state must make credible commitments to attract long-term investments of capital and labor, and if constitutional commitments are the most credible commitments that the state can make, the state then faces a clear incentive to substitute constitutional policy for conventional policy.... A government that respects no limits on its power may be hoist with its own petard when it comes to making credible commitments. The credibility of the Chinese government's efforts to reduce investor uncertainty by establishing property rights, for example, is surely undermined by that same government's wanton disregard for human rights.

"There is no firewall between constitutional law and other domestic law. Globalization cannot drive the content of government policy without also guiding the end of constitutional law."

The actions of the Federal Reserve and FDIC threaten world-confidence in the United States as a nation in which to invest capital. When the constitutional rights of individual Americans are violated by their own government, or when the positions of advocates of a "living constitution" are accepted by the United States Supreme Court,[175] then the United States as a sovereign nation can be perceived worldwide as being on a downward, slippery slope. Impeachment of radical and dishonest federal judges has been accomplished several times before, and impeachment of U.S. Supreme Court judges who advocate globalism and corporatism and who otherwise violate the principles of the Constitution should be attempted by a new Congress and every new Congress until those judges are removed from the bench and constitutional judges who take their oaths seriously are appointed.

But most importantly, the Federal Reserve must be audited and then abolished. Abolition of the Fed can be accomplished in the same manner that President Andrew Jackson did with the Biddle Bank, which at the time was the nation's central bank. In Jackson's time, the US Treasury bypassed the central bank and deposited the public tax dollars into the state banks. Similar actions today could force the Federal Reserve to pay off most of the national debt it has incurred on its own in violation of the US Constitution, instead of the US Treasury and taxpayer paying the debt. Without the tax dollars to spend, the Federal Reserve will be forced into bankruptcy like any other large private corporation, and bankruptcy court is where the nation needs to pick the bones clean of the Fed's hidden assets.

Mr. William Greider harkens us back to a time of similar financial trouble in American history—trouble that was finally resolved by abolishing the central bank:

> "Andrew Jackson built the Democratic Party around the question of whether a central bank was compatible with American ideals. Popular will—'the real people,' as Jackson called them—agreed with him. A central bank meant 'control would be exercised by a few over the political conduct of the many by first acquiring that control over the labor and earnings of the great body of people.' In 1832, President Jackson vetoed legislation to keep the Bank of the United States alive. The following year the Treasury withdrew its funds from the Bank and deposited the money

148

in a number of selected state banks, and the nation returned to 'free banking' and unfettered economic development. Optimism won in Jackson's time. 'Jackson Democracy' was a powerful set of ideals, all derived from essential elements of the American spirit—the ambitious striving of individual enterprise, the celebration of productive labor over finance, an enduring suspicion of centralized power and, above all, the yearning for a new kind of society in which every citizen would be his own master, beholden to no other.[176]

"South and westward, more distance from the eastern Establishment, state banks were less fastidious in their lending practices, more eager to believe in the potential of new ventures. The money-center banks, defenders of the already established wealth, naturally depended on order. Provincial bank failures were commonplace, confirming the conservative caution of the East. But the looser credit standards on the frontier made possible the great leaps of development—entrepreneurial dreams that came true and bankers who were rewarded handsomely for blind faith. In modern politics, the regional conflicts became muted as the financial system developed its national scope, but the tension was still present beneath the surface, in a Texas oil boomer's resentment of big-city bankers, in the Middle West's paranoia about eastern dominance, in the small town banker's complaints about Fed favoritism toward the largest banks.[177]

"When Biddle's Bank of the US was stripped of its powers, the results were dynamic. Without the Bank's overarching control of money and credit, a vast boom developed— followed by a surge of inflation and eventually economic contraction. The fears of the Eastern bankers were dramatically fulfilled. European wealth was lent to develop America and America defaulted massively, many times. In the eyes of the Eastern Establishment, a promising monetary system was destroyed, state banks were freed from federal control, and rampant speculation was encouraged. The consequence, in the eyes of the Establishment, was a 'reckless, booming anarchy.' But the country developed much faster than the cautious bankers of the East had imagined. A wild economic boom developed, fed by a dizzying generous creation of money and credit, created by the banks 'more or less out of nothing.' Without Biddle's Bank to inhibit them, the decade of the 1830s, even with its excesses, became a time of extraordinary development— gambles that mostly paid off and permanently advanced the economic structure of the nation. More than three thousand miles of canals were built between 1816 and 1840—almost two thirds during the thirties. Railroads were built, and the transportation systems linked markets and allowed the division of labor to progress to a higher plane. 'Reckless, booming anarchy' produced fundamental progress. It was not a stable system, racked as it was with bank failures and collapsed business ventures, outrageous speculation and defaulted loans. Yet it was also energetic and inventive, creating permanent economic growth that endured after the froth had blown away. The whirlwind creation of credit, wasteful as it was, had the effect of transferring purchasing power from the passive elements in the economy to the activists. The bankrupt enterprises and the bankrupt states, the 'reckless, booming anarchy'—in fact rang a joyous chord in the American character. It sounded hopeful, creative, free. Positive thinkers could shape their own destinies. It was very American—self confident and forward-looking and, on occasion, cocky."[178]

∻ APPENDIX ∽

ENGINEERS
AUSTRALIA

29 January 2009

Korea FTA Taskforce
Department of Foreign Affairs and Trade
R. G. Casey Building, John McEwen Crescent
BARTON ACT 0221

Dear Sir/Madam,

Engineers Australia is the peak body for engineering practitioners in Australia and represents all disciplines and branches of engineering, including information technology. Engineers Australia has over 84,000 members Australia wide and is the largest and most diverse engineering association in Australia. All members are bound by a common commitment to promote engineering and facilitate its practice for the common good.

Engineers Australia has invested a large amount of time and energy in developing and facilitating trade in engineering services at a multilateral level through the APEC Engineer Register, the Washington Accord and other international engineering agreements.

In most countries, engineering is an "accredited" profession and as a result, engineers are required by law to be licensed before they provide professional services or use the title "professional engineer". Many other professions such as accountancy and legal services are also subject to accreditation or licensing requirements.

These licensing requirements can often operate as significant barriers to trade in professional services. This is because in addition to having professional qualifications, licensing requirements contain other conditions such as completing practical training, passing examinations and meeting language, good character and reputation, citizenship or residency conditions.

While several countries including the United Kingdom, Denmark, Australia, Switzerland and Finland have no, or very limited legal restrictions on the provision of engineering services, the US, Canada, Japan and Singapore operate more restrictive licensing procedures.

The removal of these hurdles will rely on increasing the international recognition of qualifications and practice competency and the negotiation of professional accreditation and reciprocity agreements. These developments are an important means for professional service providers to gain international market access. This is why government support of the work already done by Engineers Australia to support international trade in engineering services is so important.

Korea, like Australia, is a member of the Washington Accord and APEC Engineer Register, which opens up opportunities to move forward on issues related to trade and engineering services under the proposed Free Trade Agreement (FTA).

Engineers Australia believes that there is scope for both the Washington Accord and/or the APEC Engineer Register (outlined further in Appendix A) to be used to facilitate the movement of professional engineers between Australia and Korea. Engineers Australia believes that the Australian government must seriously consider mechanisms within the FTA to include the Washington Accord and/or the APEC Engineer Register as the assessment framework for the recognition of university qualifications and the movement of professional engineers between Australia and Korea.

Overall, given that an assessment process already exists to recognise university qualifications under the Washington Accord and engineering registration/licensure internationally under the APEC Engineer Register, it would extremely disappointing if DFAT failed to look for future opportunities to support these agreements.

While Engineers Australia has limited resources to devote to bilateral trade facilitation we would be willing to pursue opportunities to build a closer level of engagement with Korea under the FTA. We look forward to discussion on these issues as the FTA negotiations progress.

Sincerely yours,

Kathryn Hurford
Associate Director, Policy

APPENDIX A: International Agreements

www.ieagreements.com

As a result of the work by Engineers Australia, accredited Australian qualifications and overseas engineering qualifications are recognised through formal agreements with engineering accreditation/registration/licensing bodies in other countries. While a number of agreements exist, those most relevant to Australia's relationship with Korea include:

Washington Accord

The Washington Accord was signed in 1989. It is an agreement between the bodies responsible for accrediting professional engineering degree programs in each of the signatory countries. Engineers Australia accredits the undergraduate engineering courses offered in Australia and is therefore the Australian signatory to the Washington Accord,

The Accord recognises the "substantial equivalence" of programs accredited in the signatory countries, and recommends that graduates of accredited programs in any of the signatory countries be recognised by the other countries as having met the academic requirements for entry into the practice of engineering. The Washington Accord covers professional engineering undergraduate degrees. Engineering technology and postgraduate-level programs are not covered by the Accord.

The signatory countries of the Washington Accord are: Australia, the United States, Canada, Chinese Taipei, Hong Kong China, Ireland, Japan, Korea, New Zealand, South Africa, Singapore, and United Kingdom. Germany, Malaysia, India, Russia and Sri Lanka are currently provisional members of the Accord. Engineers Australia is also currently supporting an application for provisional membership by China.

APEC Engineer Register

The APEC Human Resources Development Working Group Steering Committee for mutual recognition of professional engineers developed the initiative for the APEC Engineer Register over the period 1997 – 1998. The intent of the APEC Engineer Register is to recognise the equivalencies in the qualifications and experience of practising professional engineers in the participating economies and to facilitate trade in engineering services between those participating economies.

The purpose of the agreement is that engineers entered on the APEC Engineer Register will be granted a high degree of mutual exemption from further assessment when practising in any of the participating economies: Australia, Canada, Chinese Taipei, Hong Kong China, Indonesia, Japan, Korea, Malaysia, New Zealand, the Philippines, Singapore, Thailand and the United States. This is not yet occurring in all member economies.

An APEC Engineer is defined as a person who is recognised as a professional engineer within an APEC economy, and has satisfied an authorised body in that economy (for example Engineers Australia), operating in accordance with the criteria and procedures approved by the APEC Engineer Coordinating Committee, that they have:

- completed an accredited or recognised engineering program;
- been assessed within their own economy as eligible for independent practice;
- gained a minimum of seven years practical experience since graduation;
- spent at minimum of two years in responsible charge of significant engineering work; and
- maintained their continuing professional development at a satisfactory level.

All practitioners seeking registration, as APEC Engineers must also agree to be bound by the codes of professional conduct established and enforced by their home jurisdiction and by any other jurisdiction within which they are practising. Such codes normally include requirements that practitioners place the health, safety and welfare of the community above their responsibilities to clients and colleagues, practise only within their area of competence, and advise their clients when additional professional assistance becomes necessary in order to implement a program or project.

APEC Engineers must agree to be held individually accountable for their actions, both through requirements imposed by the licensing or registering body in the jurisdictions in which they work and through legal processes.

The APEC Engineer Register can also work as a framework for the development of bilateral mutual recognition agreements. This process has developed out of frustration that engineers entered on the APEC Engineer Register have not yet been granted a high degree of mutual exemption from further assessment when practising in any of the participating economies. Engineers Australia has successfully negotiated an MRA with Japan under the APEC Engineer Register framework.

Engineers Australia has also negotiated MRAs with Canada and the Texas Board of Professional Engineers separate to the APEC Engineer Register. More details can be provided on these negotiations and MRA outcomes if required.

❧ END NOTES ❧

CHAPTER 1

[1] Watson, Steve. "Election Fraud Worries Already Rampant: Widespread Reports of Machines Flipping Votes." http://www.prisonplanet.com/election-fraud-worries-already-rampant-widespread-reports-of-machines-flipping-votes.html.

CHAPTER 2

[2] Paul, Ron. *The Revolution: A Manifesto.* Grand Central Publishing, New York 2008.

[3] Paul Warburg, Council on Foreign Relations and architect of the Federal Reserve System, in an address to the U.S. Senate on February 17, 1950.

[4] Rand, Ayn. *Atlas Shrugged.*

[5] Goldwater, Barry. *The Conscience of a Conservative.* Victor Publishing/Publishers Printing, 1960.

[6] *The Manchurian Candidate*, United Artists, 1962. Based on the novel by Richard Condon.

[7] Brooks, David. "Obama as the fighter spells defeat for the Democrats," *Austin American Statesman*, October 27, 2011.

[8] See Chapter 14.

[9] Silverstein, Ken. "Making Mitt Romney: How to fabricate a conservative," *Harpers*, November 2007.

[10] Bingham, Amy. "Herman Cain Tells Wall Street Protesters to 'Blame Yourself,' " *ABC News*, October 5, 2011.

[11] Rother, Scott. "A Newt Gingrich Update," LessGovIsTheBestGov.com," May 2011.

[12] "A Newt World Order? The real Newt Gingrich." http://embedr.com/playlist/a-newt-world-order-the-real-newt-gingrich

[13]Maldonado, Elisha. "Chris Christi for President," *Truth Frequency News*, September 29, 2011.

[14]Goldwater, op. cit.

CHAPTER 3

[15] Embry, Jason. "Perry jumps to front of pack – now what?", *Austin American Statesman*, August 28, 2011.

[16] Confessore, Nicholas, (*New York Times*). "Lines blurring between presidential candidates, super Pacs," *Austin American Statesman*, August 28, 2011.

[17] http://www.enemieslist.info/list1.php.

[18] Dean, John (August 16, 1971), "Dealing with our Political Enemies." White House Memo.

[19] Herman, Ken. "Who is this antagonist of Perry's?" *Austin American Statesman*, August 28, 2011.

[20] Alexander, Kate. "Perry's politics, business at odds," *Austin American Statesman*, September 2, 2011.

CHAPTER 4

[21] http://www.takebacktexas.org.

[22] Wiseman, Paul. "NFIB calls Texas' business margin tax a 'lose-lose' situation," *Midland Reporter-Telegram*, April 6, 2011.

[23] Haurwitz, Ralph K.M., R.G. Ratcliffe. "Sharp likely pick for A&M," *Austin American Statesman*, August 14, 2011.

[24] 24/7 Wall Street. "Poverty's Not Just for Cities: America's 10 Poorest Suburbs," *AOL Daily Finance*, August 16, 2011.

CHAPTER 5

[25] Embry, Jason and K. Alexander "Perry talk of treason draws ire," *Austin American Statesman*, August 17, 2011, p. A1.

[26] Hallow, Ralph Z. "Bush aides' sniping exposes a Texas rivalry with Perry," *The Washington Times*, August 16, 2011.

[27] Kuhner, Jeffrey T., and J.T. Kuhner. "Kuhner: Obama's worst nightmare," *The Washington Times*, August 18, 2011.

28 http://www.phrases.org.uk/meanings/speak-of-the-devil.html.

29 From J. K. Rowling's character-Olivander the wand-maker in "Harry Potter and the Sorcerer's Stone." Warner Brothers.

30 http://www.campaignforliberty.com/article.php?view=1077.

31 http://www.youtube.com/watch?v=eF6ruaVV4Ak&feature=related.

32 http://www.youtube.com/watch?v=HESvK6cInvY&feature=related.

33 *Rasmussen Reports.* "Election 2012: Barack Obama 42%, Ron Paul 41%," April 14, 2010.

34 *Rasmussen Reports.* "Obama 41%, Ron Paul 37%", July 22, 2011.

35 Haelle, Tara. "Generation 9/11," *Austin American Statesman*, August 21, 2011.

CHAPTER 6

36 From a commentator (Bankerrkt) on a *HuffPost Social News* article titled "Black Unemployment Surges to Highest Level Since 1984," based on Annalyn Censky, "Black unemployment: highest in 27 years," *CNN Money.com*, November 2, 2011.

37 Greider, William. *"Secrets of the Temple: How the Federal Reserve Runs the Country."* Simon & Schuster, Inc., 1987. William Greider was formerly assistant managing editor for *The Washington Post*. He writes about national affairs for *Rolling Stone*. Greider interviewed Paul Volcker and other Federal Reserve governors and Reserve Bank presidents and employees, including James H. Oltman, general counsel of the New York Federal Reserve Bank; John Paulus of Morgan Stanley; Daniel Brill, retired research director; Merritt Sherman, retired secretary to the Board of Governors, and Robert A. Johnson, a staff economist in Washington. He also interviewed William M. Isaac of the Federal Deposit Insurance Corporation on October 22, 1985 and November 14, 1985.

38 Greider, op. cit., p. 255-256.

39 *America: Freedom to Fascism – Director's Authorized Version*, http://video.google.com/videoplay?docid=-1656880303867390173#.

40 Griffin, G. Edward. *"The Creature from Jekyll Island,"* 5th edition, American Media, P.O. Box 4646, Westlake Village, CA 91359-1646.

41 Johnson, Roger (1999-12). *Historical Beginnings… The Federal Reserve.* Federal Reserve Bank of Boston.

42 Known sources for this chapter and following chapters in addition to those named are: "The American Presidency Project, Jimmy Carter, Depository Institutions Deregulation and Monetary Control Act of 1980 Remarks on Signing H.R. 4986 Into Law"; Mullins, Eustace. *The World Order: The Rothschilds*; Stephen Pizzo, M. Frickler and P. Muolo, *Inside Job: The Looting of America's Savings and Loans*; FDIC, *The S&L Crisis: A Chrono-Bibliography*; Chudleigh, J.P., *Austin American Statesman.*

43 Auerbach, Robert D. *Deception and Abuse at the Fed: Henry B. Gonzalez Battles Alan Greenspan's Bank.* University of Texas Press, 2008. Robert D. Auerbach was an economist with the US House of Representatives Financial Services Committee for eleven years, assisting with oversight of the Federal Reserve. He participated on the investigation team of the Federal Reserve under the late congressman Henry B. Gonzalez (D-TX, chairman, 1989-1994 and ranking member until 1999); assisted by former congressman James Leach (R-IA; chairman, 1995-2000) who provided funds for the Gonzalez investigation. Henry B. Gonzalez was a Democratic member of Congress from San Antonio, Texas. He was elected to fill a vacancy caused by the resignation of Congressman Paul J. Kilday. He was reelected eighteen times, serving from 1961 to 1999.

44 Auerbach, op. cit., p. 4-5.

45 Auerbach, op. cit., p. 93.

46 "Money Rules: The Role of the Federal Reserve." Filmed January 9, 2002. Host: Peter Robinson for *Uncommon Knowledge.* Guests: Michael J. Boskin and Janet Yellen.

47 President Clinton signed the repeal of Glass Stegall in 1999. The Glass-Stegall Act had provided that banks should function like banks, brokerage houses should function like brokerage houses and each ought to limit its respective activities to functions traditionally falling under those respective labels.

48 Auerbach, op. cit., p. 240.

49 Auerbach, op. cit., p. 186.

158

[50] "Internationally, the approach that Senator Obama proposes—including the media magic of meetings between heads of state—was tried during the 1930s. That approach, in the name of peace, is what led to the most catastrophic war in human history." From Thomas Sowell: *An Old Newness*, April 29, 2008. Sowell is a Rose and Milton Friedman Senior Fellow at The Hoover Institution, Stanford University and author of "Basic Economics: A Citizen's Guide to the Economy."

[51] Moore, Stephen "Why Americans Hate Economics." *The Wall Street Journal* - Opinion, August 18, 2011.

[52] Hurt, Harry III; "Quick Study: Dollar Doldrums." *Readers Digest*, September 2008, p. 158.

[53] "Money Rules: The Role of the Federal Reserve," op. cit.

[54] Auerbach, op. cit., p. 4-5.

[55] From Auerbach: Martin was viewed as an ally of Truman, who opposed Fed independence; however, Martin negotiated an agreement between the Treasury and the Fed called the 1951 Accord that granted the Fed independence. Chairman of the Fed Board of Governors McCabe resigned, conditioning his resignation on the requirement that his successor be acceptable to the Fed. Trusting Martin to undo the agreement that had granted independence to the Fed, Truman selected Martin to replace McCabe and the Senate approved his appointment. Contrary to Truman's expectations, however, Martin guarded the Fed's independence through the Truman administration and subsequently through the four administrations that would follow. Some years later, Martin happened to encounter Harry Truman on a street in New York City. Truman stared at him, said one word, "traitor," and then continued. Council of Economic Advisors chairman Leon Keyserling said later "(Truman) was as strong as any President had ever been in recognizing the evils of tight money… He sent Martin over to the Treasury to replace McCabe. Martin promptly double-crossed him." From Hetzel, Robert L. and R.F. Leach, "The Treasury-Fed Accord: A New Narrative Account." Federal Reserve Bank of Richmond. *Economic Quarterly* Volume 87/1 Winter 2001. P. 33 – 55.

[56] *America: Freedom to Fascism* – Director's Authorized Version, http://video.google.com/videoplay?docid=-1656880303867390173#.

[57] FOMC Memorandum of Discussion (MOD), February 13, 1962, 62; copy sent to House Banking in 1976. Charles A. Coombs was the vice president in charge of the Foreign Department of the New York Fed Bank and special manager of the System Open Market Account. Cited by Auerbach p. 70, footnote 41.

[58] FOMC MOD, February 13, 1962, 71. Cited by Auerbach, p. 70 footnotes 42, 43.

[59] William McChesney Martin, Jr. was succeeded in 1970 by Arthur F. Burns. Martin continued to work, holding a variety of directorships for a group of nonprofit institutions, such as serving on the board of the Rockefeller Brothers Fund.

[60] Auerbach, op. cit., p. 70 footnote 44.

[61] Auerbach, op. cit., p. 88.

[62] W. Lee Hoskins, president of the St. Louis Fed, told Fed officials in 1989:" …Mexico needs $3 to $5 billion per year for the next several years…. The concern is that we would be subject to being viewed as perhaps circumventing Congress by working more closely with Administrations down the road on this kind of activity…So, whatever the general merits may be of making loans to Mexico, I don't think we should be involved without explicit Congressional authorization, Mr. Chairman. So I would oppose an increase in the swap line." (The "swap line" is the general name given to the Fed's so-called "reciprocal currency transactions". From Auerbach, op. cit., p. 66.

[63] The Fed apparently began its loans or "swaps" to Mexico about 1976, and continued the practice in 1982-1983, 1986, and 1988. From Auerbach, op. cit., p. 72.

[64] Auerbach, op. cit., p. 65-67.

[65] Auerbach, op. cit., p. 80.

[66] Auerbach, op. cit., p. 74-75.

CHAPTER 7

[67] Paul Volcker reportedly denied this later.

[68] Greider, op. cit., p. 68.

[69] *Texas Business*, October 1983.

[70] Chudleigh, J.P. Letter to the Editor, *Austin American Statesman*; The American Presidency Project, "Jimmy Carter." Depository Institutions Deregulation and Monetary Control Act of 1980 Remarks on Signing H.R. 4986 Into Law.

[71] Pizzo, *Inside Job*, op. cit.

[72] FDIC. "The S&L Crisis: A Chrono-Bibliography."

[73] "Alex Jones Protests Texas Governor Rick Perry," video.

[74] O'Grady, Mary A. "Americas: Fallout from the Fed", *Wall Street Journal*, 2008.

[75] Greider, op. cit., p. 429.

[76] Greider, op. cit., p. 484. Jesus Silva Herzog was the finance minister of Mexico who met regularly with Paul Volcker to discuss the fact that Mexico was going broke. Mexico owed $80 billion to foreign creditors, the largest share to the major American banks. Citibank and continental Illinois each had lent more than $100 million. When loan payments fell far enough behind, the debt had to be written off. Citibank, Bank of America and other would be instantly imperiled. When Silva met with Volcker, he did not threaten default nor did he need to. Fed Governor Henry Wallich, the former Yale professor, had Silva as one of his students in international economics. (From footnote 28): The most intimate account of behind the scenes discussions surrounding Mexico's financial crisis was reported by Joseph Kraft, "The Mexican Rescue." *Group of Thirty*. 1984.

[77] In 2008, due to the drop in oil prices, the Saudis announced that they would impose an $80 per barrel "price floor".

[78] Greider, op. cit., p. 517-520.

[79] Greider, op. cit., p. 545.

[80] Greider, op. cit., p. 378.

[81] Greider, op. cit., p. 635.

[82] Greider, op. cit., p. 668-669.

[83] Greider, op. cit., p. 651.

[84] Greider, op. cit., p. 653.

CHAPTER 8

[85] "Invisible Empire: A New World Order Defined."
http://www.youtube.com/watch?v=NO24XmP1c5E.

[86] http://video.google.com/videoplay?docid=-1656880303867390173.

[87] YouTube video. "North American Union & RFID Chip Truth."
http://www.youtube.com/watch?v=vuBo4E77ZXo.

[88] From Meyer. *A Term at the Fed.* p. 98, cited by Auerbach, op. cit., p. 83.

[89] Auerbach, op. cit., p. 83.

[90] Greider, op. cit., p. 621.

[91] Greider, op. cit., p. 617-618.

[92] Greider, op. cit., p. 645.

[93] Calderone, Michael. "Fox News Chief Roger Ailes thinks Sarah Palin is 'stupid'." *New York Magazine.* May 22, 2011,
http://www.huffingtonpost.com.

[94] "Rupert Murdoch and Fox News are in business with 'Terror Mosque' Imam's Principal Patrons", *DemocraticUnderground.com*, August 21, 2010.

[95] McKee, Debbie. "Join Texas activists this Labor Day weekend." *We Texans* email, August 25, 2010.

[96] Hornberger, Jacob G. "Debra Medina, Glen Beck and the Northwoods Truthers." http://mwcnews.net, February 12, 2010.

[97] Alinski, Saul. *Rules for Radicals,* 1971.

[98] "Rick Berry and Glenn Beck: Live in Concert," *PoliTex*, April 22, 2010

[99] "Ron Paul Revolutionaries Abandon Beck in Droves; Ratings Hit 2010 Low," *Daily Paul,* April 16, 2010.

[100] Wolff, Michael Wolff. "Who's really giving away Rupert Murdoch's money," http://www.huffingtonpost.com, August 19, 2010.

[101] Calderone, op. cit.

[102] Griffin, op. cit.

[103] Calderone, op. cit.

[104] Watson, Paul J. "Fox News Dirty Tricks Against Ron Paul No 'Mistake'." *Prison Planet.com*, http://campaignforliberty.com, February 17, 2011.

[105] From Greider, op. cit, p.670: "There was one other explanation most victims in Iowa and elsewhere did not wish to face – that the American political system itself had decided their fate. The deflation destroying American farmers and other producers was not imposed by remote conspirators, but by their own government in Washington, with the approval or acquiescence of their own elected representatives....It was the necessary consequence of the economic logic pursued by those who held legitimate political power in the American system, most particularly the Federal Reserve but with the tacit consent of others".

CHAPTER 9

[106] http://info.tpj.org/reports/pdf/perryprimer.fin.pdf.

[107] http://www.crewsmostcorrupt.org/about.

[108] Powell, Jim. "Welfare Corruption in the New Deal." *The Future of Freedom Foundation - Freedom Daily*, January 1, 2010.

[109] Paul, Ron. "Socialism vs. Corporatism", *Campaign for Liberty*, April 27, 2010.

[110] Price, Asher "New York's waste may make Texas a top dump." *Austin American Statesman*, February 8, 2009, p. A1.

[111] Paul, Ron. "Socialism vs. Corporatism", op. cit.

[112] Mann, David. "Slush Fun: At least one Texan has benefitted from Rick Perry's Enterprise Fund." *Texas Observer*, March 11, 2010.

[113] Duncan, Mark. "Perry's Enterprise Fund to Countrywide: "Free Money!" *Burnt Orange Report*, January 23, 2008.

[114] Embry, Jason and K. Herman. "Texas Enterprise Fund: A&M grant skirts panel." *Austin American Statesman*, March 27, 2009, p. A1.

[115] Slater, Wayne "TABC chief, a Perry appointee, solicits donations for governor." Dallasnews.com, *The Dallas Morning News*, October 22, 2009.

CHAPTER 10

[116] "International Law – Liberalism." Encyclopedia of the New American Nation.

[117] Greider, op. cit., p. 426.

118 Greider, op. cit., p. 429.

119 "Ramshaw, Emily and M. Stiles. "Doctors Without Borders." *The Texas Tribune*, May 11, 2010.

120 *Rasmussen Reports.*

121 Rosser, Mary Ann. "Head of Texas Medical Board resigns, takes position on another panel." *Austin American Statesman*, December, 2008.

122 "Doctors Sue Texas Medical Board for Misconduct – Cites institutional culture of retaliation & intimidation", Association of American Physicians and Surgeons, Inc., December 21, 2007.

123 "District Attorney asked to investigate Texas Medical Board officials." Association of American Physicians and Surgeons, Inc., November 10, 2007.

124 "Ramshaw, op. cit.

125 Heflin, Jay. "Health reform threatens to cram already overwhelmed emergency rooms." *TheHill.com*, May 15, 2010.

126 Ackerman, Todd. "Texas doctors opting out of Medicare at alarming rate." *Houston Chronicle*, May 17, 2010.

127 M. Ward, K. Alexander, T. Eaton, "Vetoes", *Austin American Statesman*, June 18, 2011, p. A7., mward@statesman.com.

128 "UT System prescribes fast track to medical practice for students," *Austin American Statesman*, June 22, 2011.

129 Kathy Medina, who also noted "As a mother of a Texas primary care physician who graduated from UT-Austin and UT Southwestern Medical Center at Dallas, I, for one, will choose the doctor who graduated the old-fashioned way." *Austin American Statesman*, Letters to the Editor, June 28, 2011.

130 "Rick Perry's ties with Merck run deep." *Associated Press*; http://www.kbtx.com.

131 K. Alexander, kalexander@statesman.com. "Bid: Tea party support may bode well for Perry in South Carolina." *Austin American Statesman*, August 13, 2011, p. A8.

132 "Rick Perry's ties with Merck run deep," op. cit.

[133] Blumenthal, Paul and J. Cherkis. "Rick Perry Super PACs Raise Issues of Coordination, Collusion." August 13, 2011. http://www.huffingtonpost.com.

[134] Blumenthal, Paul and J. Cherkis, op. cit.

[135] Nation Digest. *Austin American Statesman*, August 25, 2011.

CHAPTER 11

[136] Thomas, Pierre and R. Esposito. "Osama Bin Laden Raid: Al Qaeda 'Playbook' Revealed." *ABC News*, May 7, 2011. Alex Jones' Infowars.com.

[137] April 19, 2011.

[138] Engineering News Record series of articles on the IH35 bridge collapse 2008 thru 2010.

[139] *Wall Street Journal*, August 24, 2010.

[140] "URS Corporation Issues Statement on Settlement of I-35W Bridge Litigation." URS – Investor Relations – Financial Press Releases, August 23, 2010.

[141] Professor Mawenya. "Corruption in engineering and construction sectors." May 27, 2005.

[142] Texas Engineering Practice Act.

[143] McConnell, Steve. "After the Gold Rush: Creating a True Profession of Software Engineering." Microsoft Press, Redmond, Wa. Superceded by *Professional Software Development*.

[144] http://www.main.org/peboard/.

[145] Maginnis, P. Tobin. "Linux Certification for the Software Professional." *Linux Journal*, Vol 1999 Issue 60es, April 1999.

[146] *IEEE-USA Today's Engineer Online*. September, 2009.

[147] "Design Lines." Tennessee Board of Architectural and Engineering Examiners, Fall/Winter 2009; "IEEE-USA Annual Report 2009," *IEEE*.

[148] "NCEES approves new PE exam in software engineering." *NCEES*. September 10, 2009.

CHAPTER 12

[149] *The Associated Press.* January 17, 2008.

[150] *San Antonio Express-News.* December 17, 2004.

[151] http://www.youtube.com/watch?v=vuBo4E77ZXo&feature=related.

[152] http://www.youtube.com/watch?v=H65f3q_Lm9U.

[153] http://www.youtube.com/watch?v=H65f3q_Lm9U.

[154] Schwartz, Jeremy. "Violent drug gang uses Austin as a U.S. base." *Austin American Statesman*, October 9, 2011, p. A1.

[155] *The Dallas Morning News*, August 18, 2006.

[156] *The Associated Press*, April 30, 2008.

[157] Editorial, *San Antonio Express-News*, May 2, 2008.

[158] Guerra, Carlos, Op-Ed, *San Antonio Express News,* January 8, 2009.

[159] The French Connection. Schine-Moore Productions. 1971.

[160] http://www.corridorwatch.org.

[161] Documents obtained from open records request.

CHAPTER 13

[162] North American Union & RFID Chip Truth. http://www.youtube.com/watch?v=vuBo4E77ZXo

[163] Calmes, Jackie. "Volcker Joins List of Obama Backers." *Wall Street Journal*, January 31, 2008. WSJ.com.

[164] Gaston, Gigi. *We Will Not Be Silenced.* http://wewillnotbesilenced2008.com/?ref=http://directorblue.blogspot.com.

[165] http://www.prisonplanet.com/election-fraud-worries-already-rampant-widespread-reports-of-machines-flipping-votes.html

[166] Langley, Monica. "Volcker Makes a Comeback As Part of Obama Brain Trust." *The Wall Street Journal*, October 21, 2008, p. 1.

[167] Raum, Tom "Obama will try to block executive bonuses at AIG", *Associated Press*, Yahoo News.

[168] "Amid AID Furor, Dodd Tries to Undo Bonus Protections in the 'Dodd Amendment' Rules." www.foxbusiness.com, March 17, 2009.

[169] Donmoyer, Ryan J. "Dodd Blames Obama Administration for Bonus Amendment." *Bloomberg.com* Updated: New York, March 19, 2009, 23:43.

[170] Turner, Trish "Sen. Wyden Points Finger at Administration over Abandoned Bonus Provision" *FOXNews.com,* March 18, 2009.

[171] Turner, op. cit.

CHAPTER 14

[172] Gaston, op. cit.

CHAPTER 15

[173] Burns, Scott. "Talking about a revolution over the U.S. economy." *Austin American Statesman,* August 14, 2011.

[174] Associate Professor Law, University of San Diego; Assistant Adjunct Professor of Political Science, University of California, San Diego. Author of "Globalization and the Future of Constitutional Law" (Draft 9/21/06 – Not for Citation). Dr. Law has granted permission to Mr. Melton to quote his work.

[175] Upon taking office, each federal official, including judges, takes this oath: "I (name) do solemnly swear or affirm… that I will support and defend the Constitution of the United States against all enemies, foreign and domestic; that I will bear true faith and allegiance to the same…. So help me God." Nowhere in this oath is a Federal judge allowed to impose a foreign court's findings or opinions. Justice Stephen Bryer has stated that the United States is changing "through commerce and through globalization…(and) through immigration", and he questioned whether our U.S. Constitution "fits into the governing of other nations." Justice Kennedy in "Lawrence v. Texas (2003) cited sources such as a committee advising the British Parliament and the United Nations. In Grutter v. Bollinger (2003) Justices Ginsburg and Breyer cited a United Nations treaty. In Atkins v. Virginia (2002) Justice Stephens succumbed to the dictates of the European Union. Cited from Phyllis Schlafly's book, *The Supremacists.* Spence Publishing Co., 2004, p. 52-56.

[176] Greider, op. cit., p. 254-255.
[177] Greider, op. cit., p. 257.
[178] Greider, op. cit., p. 258-260.

www.ingramcontent.com/pod-product-compliance
Lightning Source LLC
Chambersburg PA
CBHW022108280326
41933CB00007B/302